CONDUIT

A Love Story Before, During, & After Life

JONNI GRAY, PHD

Library of Congress Cataloguing-in-Publication Data

Gray, Jonni.

Conduit : a love story before, during, & after life / Jonni Gray, PhD

1. Gray, Jonni, 1960 2. Spiritualism. 3. Channelling. 4. Future life I. Title

ISBN-13: 978-1499731064

ISBN-10: 149973106X

CONTENTS

PREFACE

On July 16th, 2012, my twenty-two year old one-and-only child, Connor, was struck and killed in a crosswalk when a distracted driver ran a red light in Salem, Oregon.

There are no accidents; there are only synchronicities. It's in hindsight, through expansive exploration, and in trusting the knowing senses, that allows us to connect all the dots and find something far more potent to make sense of it all.

Connor's transition is not the purpose for writing this book. But it is the change of his form that allowed the greater love story to be understood and shared: a soul-to-soul love story that transcends physical life.

It's often said that love is the only thing that's real in life, and it is. Yet love is more than just life, more than just the binding of our lives. We need to think outside the life-only box, the physical, three-dimensional-only box. We need to broaden our perspective of not only what life is, but the realization that we are so much more *than* life, so much more than a living physical being in this focused lifetime. Or any other lifetime. It's more than simply about life.

Love is more than personal. Love is universal, immortal. To live our current life connected to that immortal love changes the very nature of how and why we live. As eternal beings, we are always connected before and beyond our physical lives. We can live extraordinary lives from that awareness and understanding when it's integrated through the heart. We have remembrances of more than just our past lives. We have remembrances of all that we are, and all that is. We have soul memory that is far more than simply life-serving.

A conduit is a connection. It is a natural channel for transmission. It's someone sending something from one to another. If my story inspires you to connect deeper to the relationships around you, to create a higher consciousness in every little thing, to honour not just life, not just the physical, but the non-physical, the greater love and reality that is inclusive of physical yet so much more, than I have done what I set out to do.

I invite you to read this intimate story, not as a voyeur, but as a participant in a greater remembering of the meaning, the purpose, and the continuation of sacred, soul love. Love doesn't begin and end with birth and death. The journey is far more reaching than that.

It was time to share this story. The whole story. Allow this love story to stir something deeper within you. Let it to expand your beliefs, resonate as truth, and give words to your eternal self.

INTRODUCTION

FOR THE MOST PART, I FORGET what it's like to be mainstream about life, death, afterlife, spirit, past lives, channelling... I forget that most people are so afraid of death, or of what might happen after death, that they hold their breath and try to pretend that death won't happen. They don't want to think about it, much less understand it, and would never consider making friends with it.

Our culture has certainly done a number on the fear of death and the afterlife. It equates death with the final failure, using phrases like "lost the battle", "taken from us", and "final resting place". It's as though living is winning and dying is losing, as though when we're alive we're working hard, and when we die we simply rest, no longer participating with people and everything else on the Earth.

Where did that nonsense come from? Church and state, power and control of the masses, and repeated myth.

I humbly thank you for choosing to read this book. I realize I'm asking you to profoundly stretch, to expand and reshape your belief system, to bring a grander viewpoint into it all. I'm pushing evolved consciousness here. Spiritual, energetic intelligence. Non-fear, at the very least.

I also realize I've personally had a lot more exposure to death than the average person, having lost my mother-figure (the grandmother who raised me) when I was eighteen, my brother, all of my sisters, my father, my mother, and now my only child. And with each of those losses, the need to understand why increased exponentially. How could it not? If I hadn't had the need to ask and know why, I would probably be reaching for whatever form of mind-and-emotion-numbing medication I could get my hands on. But as I've always said, "meditate or medicate".

So in a deep, meditative state, I ask why they chose to live and die in that particular way and at that particular time. The answers soothe my nervous system, stretch my spiritual awareness, lock in place some valuable insights, and change the way I see life and death. They change the way I live. And all for the better.

As a past life regression therapist, I ask the very same questions whenever I do inner journeying work with a client. Whether in a past life regression or a channelling session, the questions and answers become the source of deeper understanding, acceptance, forgiveness, and peace. It's where the great revelations come from, and where the tears of truth flow from.

We are complex beings, no doubt about it, and asking why is our favourite question. Our inquisitive selves ask, "Why do we do this? Why don't we do that? Why can't we stop this? Why can't we start that? Why did that happen?" The list is endless.

Most people get stuck when they think they have to get quiet and go inside themselves to access the answers to their "why's". When they are in their greatest fear or pain, asking why by themselves can often be more painful or fearful. I understand that. I am forever in gratitude to Cheryl and Sage Council (I will introduce them later in the book) for their access and availability during my times at the bottom of the emotional ocean.

As an expert in consciousness studies, an inveterate explorer of the inner realms, I know that asking our *thinking* brain "why" is not the best approach to take if we really want the most satisfying and complete understanding. The answers to the biggest, most emotional "why's" aren't on the surface of our thinking brain. To access those answers, we need a gentler approach. We need to neutralize the emotions in order to get underneath and find out what's really triggering them. The emotions are just the tip of the iceberg.

The gentle approach is called deep meditation and spiritual connection. It's the process of inter-dimensionally expanding to our multidimensional self. Asking "why" in that state yields the experiences and expansive answers we really need to satisfy those very human "why's".

Being a compassionate guide for others in my work means I help them access the most expansive states of consciousness where the answers are understood, whether the "why's" are about death, birth, marriage, divorce, addiction, abandonment, purpose, or anything else. Together, my clients and I create the next level of freedom and joy so they can form more intimate, soul-enriched relationships with themselves and others.

I believed in the greater reality more than anyone I knew. I worked in it, lived my life based on it, took it to my core. It was my operating system for life. But only when my son Connor transitioned, did I get to the next level of living in this greater reality. The veil is really very, very thin. Anyone who has physically incarnated on the planet is energetically connected to the people they love, and to the earth, indefinitely. Yet it is through the contrast of love and loss that humans can become aligned with their souls, and therefore enlightened. I was not only privileged to have the purest soul-to-soul relationship in this lifetime, but I was also able to spend twenty-two years with my spiritual guide, Connor, while he was in physical form.

Our immortal spiritual self is more real than anything we perceive in this physical realm. Death doesn't stop love. It doesn't take away relationship. Connor is free and blissful. He radiates serenity, compassion, and wisdom. He is in the love, and death is no match for love. I feel enriched by loving Connor, instead of feeling deprived by the loss of his form.

Because Connor was so connected to those qualities when he was in physical form and I became so used to communing with him, the communication signal, since his transition, is not a lot different. He's much more than the personality he once was, but that's why he's still Connor. He's simply been upgraded - expanded - to Connor 2.0.

Now, in our choice of separate realms on either side of the veil, we are still together, and soul-to-soul love is still the meaning and purpose.

CHAPTER ONE

THE DAY

WHEN I FIRST RECEIVED THE CALL that my twenty-two year old son, Connor, had been struck and killed in a pedestrian crosswalk by a driver who ran a red light, I had two parallel experiences. One was physical and reactive, the other visceral and subtle.

In painfully slow motion, my body bent over as though kicked in the stomach. I gasped for air and backed up until I hit a wall.

At the exact same time a shadowy energy bubble that felt as though it had been buried deep inside me for eons bubbled up to the surface of my being and popped open as a full memory, a déjà vu feeling, a knowing that this was always going to happen, an absolute inevitability.

Because I was experiencing both responses at the same time, the split had me reaching for a chair. I needed to sit down. I needed the chair to ground me before I fell onto the floor. I was dizzy, and as the news and experience of it pierced through me, I couldn't find the thread of the expected emotions of shock and pain. Instead, a calm, orderly energy enveloped my senses. I felt completely still, even though my physical body began trembling as though the temperature had suddenly plummeted.

I could feel my husband, Blake, my son's stepfather for the last four years, grasping to hold it together and be my rock. But his eyes were hollow, revealing his obvious shock and powerlessness. Instead, those same eyes plunged deeply into mine, as though looking for my sense of knowing to anchor him.

We were both up early that morning, before the call. Blake was packed to take a flight out of the country, and I was completely surrounded by boxes, having moved into our new home in Roberts Creek just two days before. Everything was in flux. Everything felt up in the air. And then the bottom fell out.

I was in no-man's land, and my calm, orderly presence took over, instructing Blake to call our niece, Desirée - a professional in the travel industry, and a seasoned traveller. She'd be the best one to take care of cancelling Blake's flight and booking another one for the two of us to go to Oregon, where my son's fatal accident had occurred. We were in no shape to organize those details. As Blake spoke with Desiree, he repeated back to me what I needed to know, but for the most part I simply sat, quiet, inward, almost emotionless.

Somehow, I felt mature. It was a strange feeling, given the circumstances, but there I was, rising to the occasion that felt as though it had always been ready to happen. This was the moment I had been waiting for, on some level, all my life. As odd as it sounds, it felt right. It felt as though it was the right time and I was in the right place. It felt right for both Connor *and* I. All these intricate senses of knowingness felt stronger than emotions. It suddenly occurred to me that I wasn't surprised, but instead - full of deep, deep love. Big love. Overwhelming love.

I came out of my internal state to hear Blake say something like, "Yes, two tickets." It was then that I felt the presence of Connor. He placed his left hand on my right shoulder, his grip firm as if he were standing behind and to the right of my seated self. He said, as clear as glass, "I'm not there; I'm here."

So with a calm breath of complete trust, I carried on the touching link to Blake and placed my left hand firmly on his, and said, "I won't be going. You and Desirée go. I'll stay here."

Blake paused. "Are you sure?"

"Yes."

My calm demeanour brokered no argument. I was clearly not acting irrationally, and Blake saw this was what I wanted.

Thinking rapidly ahead, Blake decided to drive to Oregon instead of fly, picking up Desirée, at her home in Seattle on the way through. Connor had been on an amazing, much-planned solo motorcycling holiday down the coast of the United States, and was only one day from returning home. Blake rationalized that he would need his truck and some pull straps in order to bring Connor's motorcycle - and Connor - back with him. There appeared no other choice.

Since Blake had his bag already packed, he simply pressed his body against mine, held it for a moment, then walked out the door, leaving me to go back to my internal state of consciousness.

I don't remember much else from that day. It was both long and short. Without Blake's physical presence to anchor me, I slipped in and out of lucidity. Sometimes my mind raced, but mostly it hovered in a kind of suspended, non-emotional zone.

I knew I had phone calls and emails to make, so, in zombie-like fashion, I began making them.

In each phone call I retold the events as I knew them, and the verbalization of it all exposed the full strength of the tears and gut wrenching sobs. I was human after all. I lost my suspended state to the verbal three-dimensional reality. I was imbalanced, and I could feel it.

After some time, a friend knocked on the door. I was obviously not in the mood for guests, but in my confusion I answered it. Feeling understandably helpless, my friend, the realtor who had sold us our new home and was with us celebrating just the night before, said she had to come. The only thing she knew to do was bring me food.

I didn't care for the bag of groceries she brought, but then she produced a locally baked strawberry pie with a heart-shaped cutout in the middle. A pie. A beautiful, serendipitous love pie. She stared at me and said she didn't know why she bought it. But I knew.

Pie was my favourite food. Connor had always known that. Many times I would get into a fit of "I NEED PIE!", and drive him to laughter and a bit of frustration. I smiled. Of course I could accept the pie. Connor knew that the only thing I *would* eat would be pie. I could feel him still watching over me, still lovingly caring for me. It's the way we always were with each other. Why should things be different now? Throughout the day, feeling his calm tender presence merged with mine, I sliced out wedges of pink-coloured pastry to put food in my belly and love in my heart.

Everywhere I roamed in our new home I bumped into stacks and stacks of boxes. I'm one of those people who love moving, love packing and unpacking, love the process of it all. Over the years Connor and I moved over twenty times to various apartments, houses, and offices, together. It was one of our things. So, slowly and deliberately I started opening boxes and began to make order out of the chaos, with Connor's presence right beside me.

If I hadn't been so enamoured with our new home I would have run away. But where would I have run to? There was no other home. The day Blake and I set foot on this property I knew it was home. I remember calling Connor in my excitement, telling him that I had finally found home. I could feel Connor beaming, so grateful to have 'mama' happy at last.

Given the reactive choices of fight-or-flight, I've always been a clear *flighter*. And now there was nowhere to go. I couldn't run to Connor: he was already *here*. I was stopped in my tracks. "No", I told myself, "You're home. Connor's with you. It's okay."

After a FaceTime video chat with Blake and Desirée in an Oregon hotel where they crashed for the night, I went to bed. Never a good sleeper at the best of times, I lay there asking Connor to "float me". I wasn't sure what "floating me" meant, but the phrase felt right. I needed him to help suspend my over-thinking thoughts, my perceived loss. I needed support or I would cave in, imploding upon myself as the night took over.

Not one to take pills or drink, I went inside myself to other resources to soothe my fragmented nervous system, to rise above the obvious three-dimensional reality, and into the multidimensional realities I knew so well.

I felt Connor float me, suspend me, hold me in an energetic blanket, and I was out.

The next morning I woke up with a Dr. Seuss quote in my head. I don't remember ever learning it, much less memorizing who said it. But still, there it was: "Don't cry because it's over. Smile because it happened." Part of me screamed, "Are you kidding me?!", but the stronger part, the less emotionally frightened part, knew it was wise truth. So I put a smile on my hollow face and got on with whatever the next day might bring. I had no resistance to anything. In my complete vulnerability, I had nothing left to resist.

CHAPTER TWO

DOWN THE RABBIT HOLE

THE WORK I'VE CARVED OUT OF BEING a doctor of transpersonal psychology, (often called spiritual or transcendent psychology), means I happily attend to aspects of it every day, and this day was no exception. Connor used to call me a workaholic. No, that's not quite right. He used to call me "Wolfie", the pet name for Wolfgang Amadeus Mozart, who he knew was so enamoured by his work that he had difficulty stopping. It was Connor's way of reminding me that there was more to living than working. As much as I loved my work, I knew he was there to help balance me. So when he would start calling me Wolfie, I listened and responded accordingly. He always had that affect on me.

As I set to work on that morning after, I did so with Connor right beside me. I yielded to his greater wisdom though. Nothing new there. Every morning I put out a daily Facebook post and a Twitter byte at 7 AM for my small but intimate group of followers. That morning I typed out the Dr. Seuss quote.

It was also time to write another newsletter/blog post. Where was I going to get that kind of creativity from? Then, right through my body, I could feel Connor nudge me to go to my archive folder of previous writings. As soon as I saw the piece I had written in 2008 but never used, I pulled it up. I remembered feeling truly inspired and writing it all down in one sitting. Today was the day I would post that writing. I had titled it 'Buried Treasures' back then. The irony got caught in my throat.

Connor always loved my writing and read every single word. Literally. He welcomed reading everything I wrote and encouraged me like a most favourite teacher. When I would find the perfect quote to go with a particular writing piece, he was as thrilled as I was. Ever my cheerleader. I remember I chose a quote by Zelda Fitzgerald, wife of F. Scott, to go with the 2008 piece, and he loved it: "I don't want to live......I want to love first, and live incidentally."

Without editing a word, I posted the piece to my newsletter and blog and knew Wolfie had finished work for that day. Then I stopped and read the blog post out loud, and found myself slipping down the rabbit hole into an underground reservoir of memories....

Buried Treasures

Sometimes having a baby makes you go crazy. Not the actual "having" part, but I mean those days and weeks and months (and years, come to think of it) afterwards. Having a baby cracked me open.

At night I'd walk into walls. In the day...I'd walk into walls. Sleep deprived, yet never deaf to my son's colicky cries, hour after hour I held him, and walked and swayed and walked and swayed. He cried if I stopped. I think I dropped him a few times, but I was too tired to know. Or maybe I dropped myself. I know I dropped all sense of pride, accomplishment, satisfaction, and appropriate hygiene. It all just melted away into exhaustion and numbness.

Yes, I was cracked open. There were no family or caregivers for physical or emotional support. A few friends would drop by now and then, but I somehow created a very isolated situation. Worst of all, I had no manual to tell me what to do.

Constantly holding my son, Connor, horizontal, one arm under his upper chest and, the other under his pelvis, was beyond backbreaking. Night after night. Day after day. It was a bad combination of sleep deprivation and hormone imbalanced postpartum depression. I was disconnected from my body, my mind, my life. So I did the only thing I know how to do: I expanded beyond the current three-dimensional reality. Naturally.

Through years of meditation, seeing and connecting beyond the three-dimensional reality of existence, I'd developed an ability to let go to an expanded state of consciousness. One might describe this as living in another world, or simply expanding the mind to embrace our greater existence. The world that we see with our eyes is only a portion of the energy of realty. And since we are beings of energy, we can journey along that path of energy. This allows us to live as we truly are, and leave our earthly presence behind during the times when our physical bodies become barriers to our greater self.

But now I couldn't just go to another world, another reality, the way I previously had. There was this new baby. I couldn't leave him - couldn't disconnect from him. Especially when he seemed to be in such pain and need. But I could disconnect from the perception of *my* pain and exhaustion. I could answer the call of the wild, like I knew how to do. And since this was something we both were experiencing, it felt as though I needed to unleash with him. Into the natural wild, with him. So I did.

My child was the first person I let my guard down for. I couldn't carry all that armour and him, so I let the armour go. Thank you, Connor.

The bond with this human - this soul - was intense from the start. Many times I forgot to breathe. The meditative states took us to a connectivity that was sometimes understandable, but more often very strange. I breastfed him a lot, and continued to do so for over five years. It added a physical quality to the meditative states. This was so much more than the reality I had known before, the reality that was either purely physical or purely multidimensional. This was a blend of those two states, a union I had never known was possible. It joined us, flowed us, like twins - joined at the heart. We slept and nourished together 24/7. My brain was on ice. My sense of order and logic were questionable. I don't remember my husband very much. I think he was around, but I couldn't say for certain. He went to work, came home, tried to stay out of the way, physically and emotionally. I couldn't blame him. I would have, if I could have, too.

I wasn't in the typical "baby-mode", all goo-goo and gaga about a baby. I've never had that kind of response to being a mother to Connor. I didn't connect to him as a baby even then. Only as a soul.

I know that none of my friends understood this type of connection for years during that time. They'd pop around our sunny, suburban rancher. Connor and I were usually in the backyard in any weather, rolling around on a blanket, cloud gazing, even if there weren't any clouds. I can't recall any conversation with my friends. Was I even able to have a conversation? I was a confirmed meditation junkie now. This was a new kind of soulful connection I had discovered. And while it existed, I surrendered to this intimacy - what choice did I have? - and the gooey, spacious feeling that I was both the world and the macro-micro view of it all. The experience satisfied me beyond words.

I needed nothing else to function. I was in the zone, floating through ribbons of love. I smiled, for no reason. Every morning I woke up beaming, clasping my hands to my heart, mouthing "thank you". To what? To whom? It didn't matter. I felt deeply and securely connected to all-that-is, to everything.

To celebrate the preciousness of life, I started baking (an act unheard of, if you knew me). In fact I opened a one-woman catering company that extended my love of life into spoonfuls of batter plumped with organic berries and grated lemon zest. Oh, I felt zesty!

Every morning I bounded out of bed with my bosom buddy Connor, moulded him into the cornflower blue baby sling I wore on my hip (and continued to wear for years), and created dozens and dozens of aromatic baked goods that I happily delivered to juice bars, restaurants, natural food markets, and any individual who would accept my love tokens. I was in bliss, and my brain was thawing just enough to begin to plan how to integrate this glorious channel of existence into a bigger life.

The first thing I did was to begin formally studying transpersonal psychology. And then I asked for a divorce.

CHAPTER THREE

LIFE BEFORE CONNOR

I DON'T REMEMBER WHEN I BECAME aware that I was being guided by a three-year-old boy. I just remember I trusted him more than anyone else. His chronological age was of no consequence. By staying completely and always present and engaged with him, both with my five senses and in the intuitive energy field I had come to trust over the years, I tapped into a primal optimism that I knew was my foundation. Primal optimism. There was no other way to put it. The only way to continue to allow this connection between the soul and human of Connor, the soul and human of myself, and what seemed like everything else, was to remain open and trusting of its influence and effects.

Every single minute in those early years I beamed and glowed bushels of love because I was with Connor, and together we became the embodiment of love: sleeping, breathing, constantly in touch. I never left his side; he never left mine. I couldn't tell the difference between where he began and I ended.

The illusion of separateness was complete. We were one. A micro world of connectivity.

There was nothing about Connor that wasn't hyper-alert and beaming love and joy. He was always the epitome of love and joy. Our family doctor called him "gifted". Others called him "an old soul". I called him my "lert-lert". He was *so* alert, so present, so tuned into everything, both physical and non-physical. It was palpable to me.

So when Connor suddenly suggested - "Why don't we get another house and live in it together? Then daddy can live in his own house and we can visit him whenever we want." - strange as it may sound, I took the advice of my three-year-old, and we moved to "another house" and visited his father whenever we wanted. No nasty divorce here. It was a respectful, caring, uncoupling.

Of course I was now in over my head as a single mom without a plan, but to me that just meant I was aspiring to things higher than my head could presently reach. And that was okay. I kept breathing, trusting this new internal guidance, and taking action. There was no turning back. At my very core I knew I had initiated life and I was going to see it through, every single step of the way. I had to prioritize what I believed was *the* all-important relationship, and I couldn't do anything to force it to happen. I had to be open to trust something deep inside that knew what it was doing.

No one used the term 'conscious parenting' back then. Yet the term resonates strongly now. I discovered that raising my son was a lot like my meditation practice. It was about giving, not getting. I couldn't get a connection; I had to give a connection. It was about being present, lovingly focused, and in sync. When I held Connor close to my breast and gave him every ounce of my senses and beyond, we melted together. That's what it felt like. And together we established the intimate relationship of our dreams.

My meditations, my spiritual connection to all-that-is, were now linked through Connor, and yielded the same feelings and had the same perspective. They did more than feed the soul. They put me in intimate connection with the soul. The collective soul. I remember knowing that I had never felt so alive and so validated in my entire life. Something woke me up when Connor was with me. And I kept waking up from then on.

It seemed a clear contrast to life before Connor, yet there were threads that wove throughout the entire tapestry. I see that now. Hindsight is crucial to gaining more meaning.

Life had been hard before Connor. I was raised on a potent mixture of complete neglect, and fierce, controlling, violent rage. Out of survival, I learned to move away from the range of the violence. I realized, later rather than sooner, that if you were within the range, you became the target. I discovered it was more advantageous to act like a vegetable, never look my family in the eye, and stay out of verbal and visual distance.

I chose instead to create an entirely new world within. Or at least I thought I created it. But really, it was a world that seemed to invite me into it. It saw me. It offered me much-needed intimacy. And because of it, I knew I was alive.

My childhood was all about escape, and I was dearly blessed to have a natural spiritual connection to keep me safe. I walked around all day with this perspective of another world. If anyone saw me it may have looked like I was constantly daydreaming. Or that I had invisible friends.

This other world was easier to access whenever I was outside in nature, for I later understood that the consistent rhythm of all things in the natural world was like a tonic for the nervous system. The trees and the water carried memories of long, slow, growth and beingness in their energy fields. Nature was safe for me. It felt predicable, reliable, and so very, very strong. The huge trees felt like brothers, sons. The sun-warmed boulders along the mountain paths were my sisters, daughters.

My feelings often took me up the beckoning mountain we had in the back of our ten-acre hobby farm. I vividly recall, with all my senses, what was going on within me. This seemingly inner world, the reality that I tapped into, was far greater in the wilds of nature. And when I let myself go, I connected with all the lovely things in it. Loving things. I could be open and free here. And so I was.

Sometimes I'd be drawn to notice a plant, or an incline, or a sound. It wasn't just things. It was the arrangement of things. How the hill was angled. How the sunlight and the leaves dappled the ferns and the moss. I'd bend down and commune with a sweet wild plant, feeling as though I were pulled deeply into it and living in its world. More than 'Horton Hears a Who', a Dr. Seuss book about an elephant who discovers an entire world within a flower. I wasn't just in its world, I was its world. The plant and all other designs seemed to be performing for me – from me.

I noted that I could move an inch and they would all adapt to my movement. Not that I was testing them. No, I was just playing with them. And they were playing with me. They let me know that I was the star of the show and they were all supporting characters. I was getting a taste of energetics, co-creation, connection, of being one with the universe, but I didn't have the learned knowledge of any of that yet.

I never knew, or needed to know, what the name of the plant was, or whether it was edible or stinging. Those were just the physical properties and I was connecting to its ethereal essence.

My perspective channel was this sagacious viewpoint. It was perfect for a girl of eight or so.

Time held no meaning. I knew dark and light and never wore a watch. The light was different than the dark and I wanted both experiences. So I had them. I stayed out all day - even though out was in. It was the place where I was accepted. I'd often stay out all night too. I just walked out the front door when everyone was asleep. I slept in the barn, with the animals, or in the hayloft, listening to the rain pelt the roof.

It was all very groovy now that I reminisce about it – it was the '60's after all – but at the time, it was my reality, the outer reflection of my deeper, inner life. I believed in its truth and in its power and never thought it was less real than the flat-line reality that existed on another level. For me, it was far more real than what was happening in my human family. That was a war zone, where the unexpected always seemed to occur. It was where the appalling actions took place and the energy lingered.

I learned to keep my full suit of armour on at all times. It was so thick I couldn't hear what anyone said. It was so bulky I could barely move when I was indoors. So I lay down a lot, mostly behind furniture or on the floor. On days when I didn't go outside, I hid. I could be very, very quiet and no one would ever find me. Not that they ever looked.

Sometimes I'd take an interesting-looking book off one of the many dark oak bookcases we had, and hungrily consume it. Not a lot of novels actually. I was inclined to read whole sets of eclectic encyclopedias. "The Encyclopedia of Religion" was one of my favourites. Or I'd read books about "real" people. I wanted to get to know this human species: how they thought, how they made decisions, what kinds of lives were possible to live.

Looking back, I must have been like an alien exploring all I could about these human beings, gleaning it from books but not yet able to move into that reality. My experiences of the most important humans in my life were so confusing that I needed some background, some context, to make sense of it all. I rarely spoke – "deathly shy" my teachers called me – so observing people and feeding on books were my sources of understandings.

I read and read and read and then would sleep behind the furniture or deep in the tall grass out in the far fields, an open book for a pillow. And the dreams. Oh the dreams! I still remember so many of them. Emotional thunderclouds. Epic, ancestral roots. Sensual journeys. Past lives. Future lives. All over the protean map. Never linear. My desire to understand and explain who I was and what I was doing on the Earth dropped me into bountiful, majestic landscapes of existences. In my reading-intoxicated state, I would be pumped for exploration, and in those precious, soft-slumbering moments of stillness I was richly rewarded. I was downloading directly into my consciousness the greatest understandings, the most profound re-experiencings and rememberings, the operating system I would use in this lifetime.

I remember those timeless times, behind the furniture, and in the wilds of nature, as vividly as if it were this morning, and the channelled divine message meditations that I create and share in my private practice are so often based on those continuing voyages.

I'm completely certain that other children go through these types of awakenings. I watch them now and catch them at it. When I was the local babysitter in the small town I grew up in, I often went to this channel of expanded spiritual reality with the children I cared for. They sensed I could, and I knew they could, and together we'd plunge in, unleashing into the depth of the wild. It was perfect, and it was also preparation for inviting others to meditate, years later. On that channel – in that meditative state – we are open enough to see and speak the highest, grandest truth directly from our soul's perspective.

What I realized was that when the flat three-dimensional-only reality was harsh, we had choices. Even as a child. Many times these choices are psychologically explained. A child might choose to leap out of their body's consciousness if they are being mistreated, or live solely in magical thinking, shunning friendships, indulging in eccentric behaviours, exhibiting suspicion, paranoia, and other aspects of a schizotypal personality disorder.

But I'm speaking about a level of consciousness that is in addition to their normal life, not as a replacement for their life. I loved school, for example. I would rather do anything at school, than be at home, but it was more than that. I loved learning, and I adored the teachers. Especially the teachers who resembled the many comforting and familiar characters I read about in all the books, with their raspy voices that smelled like lipstick when they bent down to look at your work. I made friends with the children who were not often seen or understood. I'd almost-silently sit beside them as though asking for permission to be in their space. Before and after school, I played till my lithe body crashed. I needed no one else.

I had this other world: this soulful connected experience. This world was born out of need, yes. My home situation forced me into survival of the spirit. When things become extraordinarily difficult, we can retreat. But meditative connection is not a retreat away from the world. It's not a numbing of the senses. It's an expansion of them. It's an experience of another level of the universe.

My choice of reality allowed me to function as a whole being at school, where I wouldn't have otherwise. It parented me, and became all members of my family, gifting me with the security and belief necessary in order to forge ahead in the world. That's the difference.

When life was tough, it would have been pointless to deny it. Running away, as much as I wanted to would have been equally pointless. I got through my childhood by seeing and living it in an expanded, meaningful way. My childhood experiences were brimming with what we would now call "reframing". My meditative channel reframed how I saw and could experience everything – macro and micro. It provided me with choice when I never knew I had any.

For many people, that choice of perspective typically happens when they are full-grown adults feeling stuck in life, rather than children stuck in childhood. That can look different, but it can still happen in the meditation zone with a greater spiritual connection.

What I knew was that if I couldn't change the flat-reality experience, I had the ability to change my perception of the experience, to lessen the emotional impact, to enhance the glimmers of hope I could feel, to welcome the extra value that my situation afforded me. And I was there. Until I lost it.

CHAPTER FOUR

CONNOR'S PURPOSE BEGINS

AS A YOUNG ADULT, WHEN THE physical reality overwhelmed the connection to a greater soul reality, I lost the plot. I never lost it completely, but it faded. It diluted as my human survival needs increased. In the abandoned years, in the tormented years, in the homeless years, the connection to that which I had so effortlessly tapped into as a child was severely weakened. Amnesia hadn't taken over completely but it wasn't until many years later that I understood the faint heartbeat still beating somewhere inside me.

I had been working in book publishing before I became pregnant. My first degree had been in English Literature so it was a natural fit to surround myself with books all day. Much easier than dealing with people, I thought. I gravitated toward all the esoteric books of course, the New Age sections, the autobiographies of fascinating people, the spiritual memoirs. Every time I read that there was something *more*, it comforted me, even if I felt as though I wasn't necessarily living it anymore.

I was still an observer of the human race, still feeling as though I was pretending to be one of them, when suddenly, I was going to give birth to one. It seemed that the faint heartbeat that had been keeping me alive and connected all those years was now growing stronger, and in physical form.

Sometime after Connor's birth, I noticed that something was propelling me to make very different choices than an otherwise rational person would make. A rational person wouldn't have taken the advice of their young child and filed for divorce. A rational person wouldn't have left a reliable secure career to embark on a non-traditional, self-employed path.

Connor's very presence in my life was affecting my world and all those I connected with. This is not completely unusual for a parent/child dynamic, but my experience appeared more complex. It wasn't other new mothers I was connecting to. I didn't even know any. I was connecting to esoteric practitioners and trainers and educators, and my knowledge base and experiences were increasing in leaps and bounds.

Because Connor's utter and compelling optimism stirred something inside me, I knew I had to step up and take on more important, valuable work. I had to show up bigger, bolder, brighter, for others. And for myself. Connor was the carrot on the string, urging me forward, but no one knew it except me. When I read over the journals I poured my heart and soul into in those early years, it was clear that I felt deeply compelled to take on a higher quality of service and contribution. And always linked with those words was the inspiration for it all: I had to do it to show Connor. But what was it? Even as I wrote out those words I put multiple question marks behind them.

Logically, how would a young boy ever need to see what I was creating and doing? A child simply needed to be loved and cared for, right? No. I knew there was something else driving this particular relationship. For some as yet inexplicable reason, Connor was deeply entwined in my work purpose on the planet. I just didn't know how or why. But I knew to put one foot in front of the other, watching for synchronicities and flow, picking up breadcrumbs along the path, until I found myself somewhere. It really was as simple as that. No real plan, no real questioning and doubting. But always forward movement. The important part was the stretching. I had to get out of my own way. I had to put my ego aside as it kept saying, "Who do you think you are?", "What do you think you can do?" Instead, with Connor literally beside me, and energetically, emotionally, and verbally inspiring me, I schooled, created, practiced, taught, and loved every minute of my new-found work.

The work I do professionally has always been non-traditional. When I began my private practice it wasn't nearly as accepted as it is now. It's come much further out of the closet and right into every day dinner conversations. Or so I hear. Armed with a masters and a doctorate in Transpersonal Psychology, I chose to specialize in meditation, and past-life regression therapy. Why? I haven't the faintest clue.

Yes, I had read countless books I found in musty second hand bookstores and libraries. And yes, I had a belief in it all. But until Connor came into my life, I had no idea I'd be switching career tracks from publishing sales rep to studying and creating a practice as a Regression Therapist and meditation creator.

When I trace it back, I can see the seeds he planted so clearly. His father and I were both in publishing in those early years, so daily shipments of galley proofs arrived on our doorstep like best friends coming for tea. Connor and I would tear open the boxes and investigate the contents. As one of his self-made games, he would give me a book as an "I love you present", and ask me to give him one in return. This exchange seemed to have no purpose other than to engage us together in fits of giggles and play acting, yet I remember when he searched through many, many boxes, as though looking for something in particular. Finding what he was looking for, he stuck an old Christmas bow on the cover and formally presented me with a galley proof of Carol Bowman's 'Children's Past Lives'. I'm sure my mouth dropped open. I remember I read it all night long. The next day, things appeared vastly different. (Thank you, Carol.)

More influences of past-life books from our local library followed, as Connor literally tossed them in my lap while 'pretending' to find a book for us to read together. Giggling all the while, he would go to a completely different section of the library, select a book, and present it to me as he slid into my open, welcoming lap. That's when he tossed me - and I later devoured - Edith Fiore's 'You Have Been Here Before', Roger Woolger's 'Other Lives, Other Selves', and Raymond Moody's, 'Life After Life'.

When I finally set up my practice, clients seemed to come out of nowhere. I felt blessed. Within a few years, Connor and I began creating workshops to accommodate the curious and open-minded. Sitting in a circle on simple "backjack" meditation chairs, we'd all join together for conscious conversations, dynamic dialogues, and modern meditations, passing around boxes of tissues to support the emotional breakthroughs, and always following every group gathering with hugs and sighs.

It was all a natural fit. I continued to expand my spiritual connection as I went along through contemplative meditation, reading, writing, and speaking, and nothing was contrived. Being in Connor's presence, surrounded by his energy field, enveloped me with a belief beyond fear. Things I would have hesitated doing before, things I would have stopped myself from living before, I now just found myself doing, living, engaging. The energy of this soul-based love propelled me forward even though I knew I wasn't leading it. As he continued to drop breadcrumbs, I continued to pick them up, following the trail and trusting, because that was the nature of our bond.

Every day Connor and I went on daily walks. We often found ourselves at a peaceful graveyard that was near our home. He preferred going there rather than the public playground. He would dawdle, wanting to walk up and down the many rows, asking me to "read what they say", as he pointed to the headstones. Then he wanted me to explain more. I wasn't sure if it was for him or for me, but I'd start talking, child-appropriately, until he'd take over and tell me about who they were and "stories" about them. The environment made it easier to talk about soul and love and the afterlife. We talked about oneness and peace and power. He wasn't asking, he was telling and listening. As far back as I can remember, Connor was always spiritually and philosophically gifted and philosophical that way. He liked this "special park", he called it, and asked to go to it daily, especially for the talks they inspired. Who was I to say no?

When Connor was about three, he told me someone else was coming. I assumed he meant a baby because he told me her name was Sage. He took an old shoebox I was using for storing small bits of toys, and told me it was Sage's box. He asked me to decorate it, so together we wrapped it up and made it special. He put the things he loved inside. "For Sage," he would say when he took his outgrown shoes, his "Thomas the Tank Engine" toy train, his petting zoo book, and dropped them into the box. Everything he no longer needed and still loved, went into the Sage Box.

I didn't think too much about it, although the name 'Sage' was an interesting one. We certainly didn't know anyone named Sage in our life. His father and I were ending our marital relationship, and as much as it was very civil and respectful, baby making was certainly not on the agenda. Still, I knew Connor was onto something. He always was. I could feel his intent. I just wasn't sure what it meant yet. I also knew to simply be patient and give it time, with no attachment to outcome. Quite frankly, with so much on my plate, the whole Sage breadcrumb was easily filed away in the back of my mind.

CHAPTER FIVE

SETTING THE STAGE

WITH CONNOR IN TOW, I MOVED out of my marital house and started seeing clients in our new home. Young Connor would often hide something in my dining room-turned-office just before I took him to Montessori school. He would giggle when he did it, as though he was hiding Easter eggs. Later I would find the treasures, although often a client would instead. The gemstones, the stuffed animals, the carved rocks, they were always things that matched the energy of the client I was serving. It was uncanny, but always welcome. The clients would laugh or smile or look around as though someone had deliberately just put that object there for them.

Those were the actions of a young knowing boy. But the soul behind the young boy's facade was operating on another level and I could feel it. I sensed that Connor was connected to the soul work I was doing in a way that I certainly didn't understand yet. But on that level, his soul energy was always present in my sessions with clients. I knew the feeling well for it was the same soul energy I had tuned into in our meditative states since he was born. It was a wise, old, feeling. A guardian angel feeling. Yes, I knew it well.

The two of us were forging ahead, creating a new and trusting life of intimacy and service, and then suddenly both my sister and father passed away within two weeks of each other. I was devastated.

Although my thirty-seven year old sister excelled physically, she was never emotionally or psychologically strong enough for this world. Certainly not strong enough to resist the lure of its lower temptations. Her addictions had become the perspective she chose, from the complicated childhood we had both had. They were the choices of my other siblings as well, but those siblings were stronger and would last a bit longer.

There are some people you sense will not live long, and you know that one day you will receive a phone call telling you they have gone. The day that call comes is no less a blow to the gut. The phone call I received that told me my fragmented sister had been killed in a car crash still knocked my wind out.

The police instructed me to the hospital morgue to identify her bruised and battered body. Her fragility was never more apparent. I just stood there, longing to breathe, unable to cry, glued to my last physical moments with her.

Later that week I placed the urn that carried her cremated ashes on the floor behind the drivers seat of my Toyota hatchback. That way, when I drove, I could keep one hand behind the seat, stroking and loving her, as I sobbed.

Almost two weeks went by and the urn was still in my car. Connor noticed, and quietly, respectfully, kept breathing for me. It was winter. The ground was too frozen to prepare a hole to bury her ashes at the cemetery. But waiting for the thaw didn't matter to me. I felt close to her while I drove. I didn't want to bring her into my home. Gypsy soul that she was, she felt most uncomfortable with people and with homes. Her comfort was in whatever second or third-hand car she could pay cash for and drive into the ground. So behind the drivers seat she rested, until I received another phone call. Another blow.

My father had hidden the symptoms of his lung cancer until it was virtually too late to do anything about it. Now, at just sixty years old, he would join my sister in an urn behind my car seat as well. When I drove with my left hand, my right hand wrapped itself behind my car seat to grace my father. When my right hand guided the wheel, my left hand soothed my sister.

The months went by. The grounds had thawed but I hadn't. Driving my car became my spiritual practice. The emotional pain was still so intense I just drove and drove. And moaned. Connor just breathed, rubbing my arm, sending love into the air. Always stoic.

It was too much, too soon. But tragedies don't always come in neatly spaced out intervals, as I would realize again, nearly twenty years later. My world was forever changed and my sense of vulnerably was at an all-time high. Connor felt it, and because of our deep bond, he got to work setting some order back into our lives.

His Montessori kindergarten teachers let me know that his coping strategy was to purposefully polish anything and everything all day: silver, bronze, gold, pewter, tin, you name it. When the teachers ran out of things in the classroom to polish, they happily brought in everything they could think of from their homes: trophies, silverware, metals, boxes, even pewter sugar bowls. If they brought it into the classroom, he would polish it.

I knew this was more than simply cheap labour, so every day, crouched behind the prickly shrubs with a spotty view into the classroom from a nearby window, I watched Connor take old sports trophies and turn them into gleaming awards. His face showed utter satisfaction even as he looked around for something else that needed polishing.

I stared through the school window at my son, my wise son, until I understood. His focus was on restoring beauty and lustre and life. He was modelling how to establish order, and I needed that guidance. I was learning from his energy, his words, and his actions. The roles of parent and child were unnecessary.

When I picked up Connor at the kindergarten door each afternoon, he would beam with pride from his day, glowing right through my grief and sadness, shining his innocence into my heart to reflect a new world. I felt the profoundness of it all. I could feel it, and soon, would see it too. My heart was open to following his lead.

That Christmas, old soul Connor found a magical collection of Victorian angel tree decorations. He looked into me and said, "Let's get them, mama. We know two more angels this year. Now we know lots." Agreeing with his perspective, I bought the angel ornaments, and together we filled our noble fir. To add to the Christmas angels, my visionary son painted dozens more pictures of the angels he told me he saw. He was grounding the angelic energy for me that year. He was connected and connecting to unseen guides and I was getting used to looking at the mature soul in a child's body, and seeing and hearing the mature soul. Even though my apartment doubled as my professional client office, I allowed angels to fill our humble home that year, covering the walls, the doors, the mirrors.

Living on our own, moving through the daily tears of the perceived loss of my father and sister, Connor showed signs of night trauma whenever the fire alarm went off in the apartment building. Like most false fire alarms, Murphy's law dictates they happen in the wee hours of the morning when everyone is deep in dream state. Living on the fifteenth floor meant I had to carry sleepy Connor under one arm, and the dog I inherited when my sister passed on, under the other. I'd hobble down the fifteen flights of cement stairs to the sights of flashing firetrucks and mobs of house-coated grumpy folk. After an hour or more we would then be instructed to walk back up all the flights, for the elevators were jammed with waiting lineups that would have taken another hour. As soon as Connor would drift off to sleep again, he would suddenly awake in tears. Again and again this happened. It was exhausting for both he and I. The fire alarms seemed to go off twice a month or so. Who was burning toast at that hour?

A pattern was emerging in Connor, and I was armed with book resources and new skills to tackle it. One night, after a trauma episode, I held him close, tenderly rubbing his back as he closed his eyes. I told him I was right beside him and that he was safe. Then I firmly and lovingly asked him what he saw and felt that frightened him.

As Connor's eyes fluttered, his focused feelings of safety, coupled with his traumatic emotions, allowed him to re-experience the visions and emotions of a past-life. In first person perspective he told me about the fire, about the other firemen, about the burning building, about getting caught in the fire, and about being on fire. Then he paused before telling me it was okay. He said he was out of the fire, and there were others there who were waiting for him. I knew he had crossed over from the trauma of that lifetime and was now in a peaceful realm.

I don't know how long I held him as he re-experienced that lifetime. Not long, I suspect. I do know that he fell deeply to sleep after that and those night-time traumas never showed up again. One day, not long after, he told me his birthmark - his port wine-like stain that covered his entire arm - was from the fire. And really, it looked like it too. Others had commented over the years, asking me if it was a fire scar. Not understanding, I always felt that was a strange question. But now it made sense. Connor carried that birthmark all his life.

Over the years Connor and I accessed dozens of his past lives for various reasons. Regression work is such a useful tool to dig deeper and find the root causes to help understand and integrate our current traumas, fears, phobias, as well as our passions and joys. Connor and I didn't go looking for greater understanding of our relationship, though. We used the regressions to smooth out his rough spots, to work on his triggered emotions, to resolve fears and traumas that got in the way of the purest love, and to connect him to his personal spirit guides so he had his own resources as he went through life. That changed everything.

It had been a full and emotional year. My heart was open; my mind was open. My physical and emotional world had quickly changed in a short period of time. The depth of my despair at the sudden passing of my sister and father had broken my heart open even more. The early years of connecting to the zone of love through this soulmate-of-a-son had prepared me for the best there was, and held me stronger and closer through the worst that was. Now I was ripe with raw vulnerability. And at the same time, prepped by Connor's careful seed planting, committed to my purposeful work. The stage was undoubtedly set.

CHAPTER SIX

SAGE COUNCIL

I HAD ALL BUT FORGOTTEN ABOUT Connor's early 'Sage is coming. We have to get ready for Sage' messages. When he spoke of Sage I was alert, as I always was, to this incredible boy's ability to be in tune with spirit. But I never linked Sage to a non-physical entity until I met Cheryl.

It was a regular client day in February, 1996, and I had already facilitated several clients in accessing their past lifetimes. Each regression worked to help them bring out their unquestionable knowingness to live their current focused life with more meaning and connection. I noted in my appointment book that a new client, a woman named Cheryl, was next.

Cheryl had found me through one of the magazines I had advertised in over the years. Like many clients, she wanted clarity on her work, her purpose, her relationships, and her life, and felt that by using the greater reality lens of other lifetimes she could gain an expanded perspective, connect some dots, and create new change. I sensed she was also interested in the process of it all. I couldn't blame her, for I have always found the subject and work fascinating myself.

Cheryl's past-life regression session began like most others until it became evident she was quickly accessing states of consciousness that were not necessary for simple memory recall. All memory is actually closer to the surface of our minds than we would think. With focus and intention, with trust and often guidance, we can access memory relatively easily. When a client moves through states of awareness rapidly, deeply entering into realms of consciousness beyond pure memory, it's a sign of channelling or mediumship - bringing through messages from non-physical beings.

As esoteric as that may be for many people, I was in the type of work that was aligned with channelled messages and mediumship. Others had channelled in my office over the years. Many clients had read Brian Weiss's "Many Lives, Many Masters" almost ten years before, and were more comfortable with the concept and experience because of it. It was all within my calling, and I was a professional. But this was different.

During Cheryl's first session, I was in the meditative zone, as I often am during the regression, until I was jolted out. Cheryl's verbal narrative was less about a past life, and more about a running stream of messages. And the messages were about both of us. This was unlike other clients, other sessions, and since it involved myself beyond the role of therapist, I found myself sitting on the edge of my straight-backed chair, tuned in, while blindly taking copious notes, and leaving my critical mind at the door.

After the session was over and Cheryl opened her eyes, I knew the whole experience had been overwhelming for her.

She was full of questions, although innocently believed that what she/we were doing was the norm. As her allotted time was up, and my next client would be waiting, I let her leave, but encouraged her to call me that evening so we could talk it over more.

That evening we discussed it for hours, and on many more occasions after that. There was a lot to process, for both of us.

Everyone *can* channel. Everyone *can* bring through messages from non-physical beings in the greater reality. But very few actually access the messages easily, clearly, and consistently. There was more going on here. It would take years to put the pieces together and even more years to own it entirely.

Cheryl and I continued to have more sessions. The information she verbalized was apparently from a non-physical group of energetic beings who referred to themselves as "Sage Council". The two of us would align our energies through a meditative state as Cheryl would speak the words from Sage Council, and I would yield to automatic writing. We asked Sage Council who they were, where they came from, what their purpose was, and a million other questions. Neither of us took their presence or messages lightly. We were both highly independent women and hadn't even formed a friendship in this life. Yet here we were, already plunging into divine messages through the ages. Like everything else that was going on in my world, it was sudden, fast, and deep.

In the early years, we probably channelled once a month although Sage Council encouraged us to access them at any time. Those messages, and the energy they carried, slowly but completely changed our lives. For years the messages were very personal and private, clearly meant to guide and council both

Cheryl and I. They prepared us to integrate all that we were on the planet today. When Sage Council's messages evolved from personal to global, Cheryl and I were told we were being guided to make the messages available to all. There's a lot of responsibility and integrity attached to such work and purpose.

Over the years, Cheryl and I noted that we could both access the divine messages of Sage Council on our own. In our writing, in our speaking, in our meditations, Sage Council came through for both of us. But when we brought our energies together and I closed my eyes and connected, and Cheryl closed her eyes and connected, the messages were amplified, more profound, with much more energy, intensity, and love.

What Cheryl and I realized was that when we met, it was really a reuniting of many, many lifetimes. Neither of us were aware of our backstory at that time, but over the years we have connected countless dots throughout the ages, and even in this lifetime. We have both recognized the sacred bond forged over those lifetimes, and the divine promise of sharing messages of universal love today. Our relationship is a connection brought forth from eons of deep spiritual alignment. Individually and together, we have chosen to serve humanity again and again. This lifetime was no different. The time to join together was now. All roads led to it.

As a conduit, Connor had foretold it, bringing me the message that Sage was coming, years before. He then gently nudged me into the line of work that would be both foundational and instrumental for the joining together of Cheryl and I in order to access Sage Council. As I looked at this little boy, I beamed with deep soul love, and realized I had given birth to my own spirit guide. It doesn't get more profound than that.

It was presented to us that Sage Council was comprised of the sacred energies of Jesus, Archangel Michael, Mother Mary, and Mary Magdalene. That confused both Cheryl and I. Over the years they have told us that they do not come through as biblical characters, but rather as "representative of divine stream energies". They explained that "the energies of the Christ Consciousness have been permeating many souls for decades", and that as Cheryl and I had spiritual guides in that energy stream they were attracted to us as channels. With the work that I was involved in, I could accept this - once I understood it. After all, I had clients channelling through their past lives, their future lives, their afterlives, and their Spirit Guide relationships, so this was really communication from another dimension, and I was very used to being in other dimensions.

Sage Council further explained that "the Christ Consciousness energy is all about unity and the power within. It's about aligning the divine feminine and masculine entities". They've told us that Archangel Michael is the "right-hand energy partner of the Christ Consciousness", and Mother Mary is "symbolic of the mother energy that mothered divine consciousness onto the planet". Balancing the Christ energy and the Archangel Michael energy, Mother Mary is accompanied by Mary Magdalene who represents the "female sexual identity; the reflection of the power of feminine fire".

Now, neither Cheryl nor I have any religious affiliation. When pressed to answer if I'm Christian, I find myself saying, "Yes, and more". I do not discount Christianity, but it's also not solely what I subscribe to. When Eastern philosophical, spiritual, native influences met up with Western influences, it started a widespread way of thinking, believing, and practicing, that we all reap the rewards of. In fact, we continually add to that bank of knowledge and experience every day. The New Age is an evolving movement, not a religion.

As a doctor of Transpersonal Psychology and as a human being, I subscribe more to the set of beliefs and principles of the New Age Movement which is in alignment with all the messages of Sage Council. The New Age Movement believes that everything is of God/Source/Love/Consciousness - or whatever you decide to call the governing energy. Those that subscribe to this philosophy believe that all is one and all reality is part of the whole. They also believe in the continuation of life energy through reincarnation, that mankind creates its own reality, and on and on.

Even though Connor was only six years old at the time we began channelling Sage Council, I told him all about it. After all, he always retained a twinkle in his eye whenever the name "Sage" was mentioned. I remember he asked me more about them, as he always did with any of my work. So on days when I was going to get together with my co-channeller, I would tell Connor, and he would often provide me with questions he thought I should ask. Always trusting his guidance, I would write them down and put them before the Council.

Sage Council confirmed all the senses I had been having all those years about Connor and I. They told me, *"Jonni, you are very blessed. Connor is a beautiful and gentle soul. On a very deep level, Connor has known that his connection to you was his alone. He is very empathic, very in tune. And he loves you so very much."*

The following year I asked them for more understanding of our choice to be together in this lifetime, stating, "We're not like mother and son."

"No", they replied. *"Not like a mother and a son. Connor is a very old, old soul. He's actually come in as your teacher. We see him as a wise old man, and he is very much your rock and your strength. He is teaching you always. In a previous lifetime he was your teacher and you were the student. You were both Asian in that lifetime. He was a Master and you were his male student. In that lifetime he taught you warrior skills, so he sees it as a cosmic joke that in this lifetime not only would you be female, but you would be his mother. He works very hard in this lifetime to remind you of that warrior male self that you once were, and this is part of the overall plan for your healing and purpose on the Earth at this time."*

It was amazingly freeing to feel the truth resonating in my body, making the hairs stand up on my arms. My knowing senses were confirmed, and with it, my circle of trust expanded to include not just Connor now, but Sage Council, and my co-channeller, Cheryl, as well.

When Connor was eleven he prompted me to ask Sage Council about his greater purpose. They told me, *"Connor's in complete alignment. There will be a challenge for you as he moves on and separates from you. We do not see that time for years yet, but we do suggest you begin preparing, as you have a very close and connected relationship with each other. We see it as being helpful to spend more time away from each other preparing you both for that eventual space and distance, but you'll always be connected spiritually and emotionally at the heart."*

I heard those words from the point of view of a parent knowing the child would one day leave the nest. In hindsight, I now see the layers of meaning, and understand the limited amount of physically-measured time I would have with him on this planet in this lifetime.

CHAPTER SEVEN

SOUL-TO-SOUL LOVE

WHEN I LOOKED AT CONNOR, the older adult looking at the younger child, I reflected to him his human power and abilities. I taught him how to be a stronger human while maintaining the trust in his intuition and internal guidance. For me, being a human being was a learned skill, but I had thirty years on him, even though those learning years still felt as fresh as wet paint.

I considered Connor my equal. He never seemed to have the need for traditional parenting. He was gentle, sensitive, wise, and able to tell me what he needed as well as what was good or not good for him. Being a vegetarian, I started him along the same path until one day he told me he could eat things that swam in the water but not things that walked on the earth or flew in the air. His words stopped me in my tracks. I hadn't thought of it that way before. But Connor saw things from a most unusual angle. It was never contrived. Always pure. So I brought fish and seafood into our diet.

I would show Connor something or tell him something and he'd question it. I liked that. He wasn't questioning me. He was questioning whether that was the best way to do something. It could be about anything: Should we move? How? By ourselves? With movers? How do we want to spend weekends? What do we want to fill our days with? Who do we want to visit? What time should we wake up? What car should we buy? Everything was up for discussion and mutual agreement. More often than not, together we figured it out. I listened; he listened. I made decisions; he made decisions.

Some people are born wise. Connor was one of those. Out of deep respect for the soul I knew he was, I took his council all the time, for I knew it be truth. It wasn't just his advice, the opinion that comes from his three-dimensional ego. It was deeper than that. Some might believe I gave too much power to the child. After all, I was the adult parent. But I knew we were in this together, and so together we'd make the very best of it. There was no need for ego power or control by either of us. There were two of us, I thought. How hard could living life be when you both were coming from a mutually respectful place?

Things got comical sometimes. Other times they were more emotional, more passionate. We developed a system when he was about nine years old. Whichever one of us felt more certain about a particular decision or choice would make the call. Believe it or not, that worked extremely well in both our favours. As a highly principled young man, if he felt he absolutely should quit a school program, I would honour his choice and accept it. I knew he was coming from a place of authentic integrity. He saw my trust of his decisions and that increased both his own self-worth and his belief in me. It worked both ways.

If he felt that I absolutely needed to purchase that new sofa (even though the cost was frightening compared with the dollars in the bank account), he would look me in the eyes until he could see that *I* was sure, that *I* had considered everything before making this decision, and he would then honour my need, and accept it.

It's not my intention to brag about him. Hero-worship is a falsehood. There is no need to put Connor up on a pedestal and make him sound better than he was. He was a humble young man, but as anyone who knew him would testify, he had an old soul and deeply compassionate presence, coupled with an extremely sharp, quick, keen mind. Like all of us though, he was flawed. He was human. And I, as his parent, was privileged with the responsibility to assist him in rising above and moving through his weaknesses and resistances. He, did the same for me. I often thought we raised each other.

Our system of mutual agreement gave him access to his confidence and abilities as he experienced the full outcome of each choice he made. For myself, our respectful system allowed me to have someone who knew me better than anyone else, be a conscious witness to my own self-trust learnings. What our system did for each other was all about validation and support. He wasn't a child and I an adult. He wasn't less than, and I greater than. We grew up together. We treated each other lovingly as equals. It was the only way our connection could thrive and expand.

Sharing everything meant sharing everything. Trust is trust, and learning curves are part of building trust. And so it was with money. Connor was so much better at managing and organizing money than I was. I would have thought that as the older, skilled human, money would have been my domain of sharing skills.

But money's a funny thing. It's more energy than physical, and Connor clearly got that sense and awareness.

When he was eight years old, he started taking over my/our finances. From trips to the accountant's, to daily budgeting, to spreadsheets on the computer, he was the one who led the way. As a self-employed business woman I had deposits to make at the end of each day, and Connor was the one to make those. I remember cluing in to aspects of his financial management when I noticed that he had been depositing a portion of each day's income into an abandoned savings account. I assumed he knew what he was doing and never felt the need to question him about it. This went on for about a year, at which time Connor announced that he had saved enough for us to have a holiday.

Never one to patronize my child, I asked him to explain it to me. I remember he talked to me about aspects of the energy of money that I wouldn't even learn about until years later when books on that subject became popular and mainstream. Somehow he understood the magic and the alchemy of money creation and management, and was modelling to me how it was done. He saw and knew money in many different forms and took conscious part in changing the forms to suit our needs. I was fascinated. That year, we went on our first of many holidays together. Thank you, Connor.

Growing up, Connor would often come up to me out of the blue and tell me about his lifetimes before he was "the Connor". He actually referred to himself as that title all his life, as though it was a role he was playing. It started as soon as he knew how to pronounce his own name. And from a very young age, he also referred to me as "Jonni". He knew my role was mother (he said it was "mama") but he called me Jonni more often than mama.

It was never done out of disrespect, or to show off his power the way others do when they discover their parents have first names other than mom or dad.

Picking him up from grade school Montessori was deafening. There were so many other parents picking up their children with the sounds of "mom, mom, mom" coming from every child. Yet clear and calm, a sweet voice would simply call out, "Jonni", and all puzzled eyes would see Connor calling on me.

His Mother's Day cards over the years would proclaim in colourful crayon or fancy felt pen: "Happy Mother's Day, Jonni!" and then underneath it, "To Mama, Love the Connor". I smiled, squeezing the little boy carrying the big messages, and accepted it all.

We always knew we were playing roles, whether the role was mother and son, or even Jonni and Connor. They still felt like roles to us and we smiled and indulged in them, especially in public or when we were with friends. When we were alone together, the masks came off to reveal the most loving, respectful, honouring relationship. It was truly such a pleasure to be his "mama", even though that was simply the common title that others understood.

Still, even within that range of mother/son, others could sense, others knew, that this wasn't your average relationship. For one thing, I rarely remember us ever arguing. There was mature communication and negotiation no matter what age Connor was, and no matter how tired or stressed or overwhelmed either of us may have been. There was no typical adolescent period, no clashing of the wills. We were each other's best friends and strongest supports, and our first and favourite choice was simply to be together. Always. As Sage Council once confirmed: *"The relationship you have with Connor is a model of love."*

Although I did not take Connor's father's last name when I married, preferring to retain my maiden name of O'Connor, I gave the name to Connor, as is often done, when a child is born. A few years after Connor and I moved into "another house" he stated that he wanted to have the same last name as me. I smiled. It didn't matter to me; it wasn't a name competition. But in some way Connor wanted to get as close as possible, to own and embrace the two of us as a unit in every way. I told him to use my last name as his - making his name Connor O'Connor - for one year, and then we'd look into doing it legally and permanently. He agreed that that was a good decision. I set it up with his understanding Montessori school teachers. Faithful to my word, a year later I gave Connor a piece of paper and pen and asked him to write out his old name. He did so, awkwardly, and passed it back to me. He had misspelled his last name. When I pointed it out, he laughed, seeing that as all part of the organic process. With his father in confused agreement, Connor proudly became Connor O'Connor. That year's holiday included time on a tropical beach. With a great sand-drawing stick in hand, Connor signed his new name as big as he could, revelling in the fact that now we both had the same name.

We went everywhere together. And I mean everywhere. I never left him with anyone except his father for even brief periods of time until he was almost four. I didn't have a need or a desire to. Unlike co-dependency, which brings out two people's worst or lowest emotions and behaviours, our relationship brought out each other's best feelings and actions. Even if I was running an errand at the drugstore or the grocery market, Connor insisted on coming, no matter how old he was. It never felt like a burden.

When he was very young and constantly wanted to be with me, I could feel why. His insecurities as a human being were reminiscent of mine, so of course I noticed them. I never indulged in them, but worked with him to strengthen his trust in himself and the universe, to remember who he really was as a fully aware soul. I would talk to him about it, and meditate with him as well. Once he established the connection through meditation with his own non-physical beings, his spirit guides, I saw the shift.

He was about ten when I watched him change. Then he *deliberately* wanted to be with me wherever I went, and it had nothing to do with fears, or loneliness, or even boredom. It felt like he wanted to be there with me, not fill in time or just hang out. He was never moody about it. He would simply state, "I just want to be with you." I understood, and readily accepted his inspiring companionship wherever I went.

In reflection now, I understand even more. Connor wanted to be with me to imprint his physical and energetic presence into the routine things one does in the day. As I go about my days now, I feel him beside me in the drug store, in the market, at the bank, on the street, while getting my hair done, and especially in the car. It's not memory. I know the difference. I'm an expert in memory. It's what I do. This was energetic imprinting designed to help me accept his presence beside me even now. It's not a great leap for me to make, because we laid down the phenomenal foundation for a lasting, living relationship whether physical or non-physical.

It went both ways, although Connor taught me by modelling it first, as he so often did. In an excerpt from a Mother's Day letter he wrote to me in 2011 when he was twenty-one, he said:

"I want to thank you for making sure that no matter how far away from me you are physically, I never feel that you're far away. You do it so well. So good in fact, that I don't really notice that you're doing all these little things like texting good morning and good night, checking in throughout the day, Skyping with me on my lunch hours and at other random times throughout the day. You do all these little things and it makes me feel like you're right here, and I just want to tell you how grateful I am that you make me feel that way.

But feeling like you're not physically far away is one thing, feeling like you're emotionally close is another, and you make me feel that way too. I always feel like we are connected even when we aren't anywhere near each other, and that takes skill for you to make me feel that way. I don't know how you do it, but some way or another I always feel that we are super close and connected.

So, happy Mother's Day, my uber-connected mama!!

Much love for eternity,

The Connor"

When Connor was young I indulged in randomly gifting him with simple but well thought out "I love you" presents. He had always liked playing that game, so I carried on with it. Contrived occasions such as birthday's and Christmases were dull. I refused to be limited by expectations of those gift-giving times. Instead, the absolute joy Connor showed for me when I surprised him made the whole experience magical. He received gifts better than anyone I knew, for he saw the soul of the person giving the gift. And to be truly seen soul-to-soul, was the *greatest* gift.

As Connor got older, his love-filled desire to cherish me, to show me my worth, meant that he too lavished me with

"I love you" presents of every kind. With immense joy, he bought me the most extraordinary gifts from his hard-earned money: hand-crafted wooden boxes, inlay frames, artisan pottery, leather-bound books, perfect kitchen appliances, the latest technological devices, extraordinary things he thought I would love for my office, and on and on. When he journeyed through Europe with a group of travellers after high school graduation he selected spectacular one-of-a-kind jewelry that made me feel every ounce of his love. Everywhere I look in my home there are gifts Connor wove into my life, and all I ever asked for were words.

"Ah yes, the traditional Mother's Day letter, generally written after a week of listening to you shout, "WORDS!!" whenever I mention the words 'mother' and 'day' in the same sentence.

Over the years I've learned one thing that stands above the rest: Mama knows best. I trust you implicitly. You are there to tell me I can. You see things I don't. You see possibilities when I cannot. You say "say yes" so I say yes. I just want you to know that I am incredibly grateful for the amazing new perspective on things that you give me and how you allow me to move forward to new things I never thought possible. Each time you teach me that I am able to move forward I register it in my mind and it becomes easier and easier for me to start to see possibilities myself. It's an amazing gift you are giving me every day. A gift that will serve me every day of my life forever. The gift to be able to move forward and to recognize an opportunity and take it. I hate to sound like a MasterCard commercial here, but that gift is priceless.

I'm sure you know what an amazing gift you are giving me, and I'm sure you know how important it is, but I want to let you know that I know it too, and I see it, and I see how it's helping me, and I'll say it again a million times or more, you are the best mama in the world.

Much love forever and always."

Connor was a class act. His respect and love knew no bounds, because, apparently, love doesn't either. He showed love in his ever-present ways, and listened better than anyone I know.

The amazing bond of love I share with Connor is truly all-consuming. It always has been. But this bond does not distract me from living a purposeful life. It's the lens through which I *live* a purposeful life.

The love was often overwhelming, as though our bodies couldn't take the high-capacity love, the finely-tuned vibration. When Connor was younger he would press his cheek to mine and we would both hum, melding into each other vibrationally. One day, when he was about twenty years old, he stopped in his tracks during our walk. Tears filled his vivid blue eyes, and this teddy bear of a young man looked right through me, into my soul, and said, "I don't know why I love you so much, but I do. I love you so, so much."

CHAPTER EIGHT

PREPARING TO LEAVE

IN HINDSIGHT, THERE WERE SIGNS that Connor was wrapping up this lifetime. There always are. You just have to look for them. And when you find the signs you weep with understanding, even though your heart feels as though it's breaking. In much the same way that bringing Connor into this life broke me open, finding the clues to confirm that Connor was leaving, broke me open even more.

I never dated after my divorce and during the years of raising Connor. I never wanted another influence to dilute our love connection nor did I want to share him on any level. As he got older, though, I knew psychologically how important it was that he see his mother happy in a relationship. I knew that it would also model the next level of his maturity and connection with another.

When I started dating my husband Blake, Connor was eighteen. I had known Blake in high school some thirty plus years before. He was the man my young heart wanted to marry, but at sixteen years old it was far more of a fantasy than a possibility. Still, I used to look into Blake's dark brown eyes and know that he was the one. My knowing senses were always right, even if time wasn't on our side yet. After high school graduation, we went our separate ways. We both had a lot of growing up and living to do before either of us were ready for the other.

When Blake found me and emailed thirty years later, I pulled my old high school annual off the bookshelf and showed Connor, Blake's picture, telling him, "He's the one I wanted to marry all those years ago." Connor smiled, calm and composed. So mature.

Just as he had talked about, and predicted, the coming of Sage Council over the years, Connor had also talked about, and drew countless pictures of, the man he referred to as the "third person". The pictures Connor used to draw of the third person made me think of Bozo the clown more than anything else, and with every picture it seemed the purpose was to try to make me laugh. It worked. The pictures of the third person always had two things in common though: he had an afro, and very strange feet. And wouldn't you know it: Blake had an afro, and the strangest bone-protruding feet. Even his foot doctor called them "the ugliest feet" he'd ever seen.

Part of Connor's plan seems to have been to make sure the right person was in place so I wouldn't be left, in practical terms, alone. The only way he would choose to exit from this lifetime would be if I were moving on in a solid relationship. So, the first thing he did was write a letter to Blake. In it he listed the "Top Ten things you should know about Jonni". I admit I was curious and a bit uncomfortable at the thought of him comprising this list. What would be on it? And why? He knew he was passing the baton onto Blake, and his dear, sweet Top Ten was a hilarious list of the oddest idiosyncrasies of mine. I won't embarrass myself here by listing even a few of them; we all have our strangeness. Connor just wanted to make sure Blake was aware of, and could handle, mine. At our wedding, two years later, Connor wrote me more words to convey his feelings, and as always, our mother/son role wasn't even a consideration in his viewpoint.

"Happy Getting Married Day, Jonni. The best ways to tell how right something feels is by how natural it is. Some things feel so right they are almost not a big deal. They don't create any huge and wild emotions. They just make you feel content inside. That's how I feel about your wedding. It is so 100% the best thing to do, I can't describe how natural it feels. I feel no sense of worry. Only pure delight. You chose well, my young Padawan. You chose a brilliant setting for a wedding. This town is undeniably beautiful and although its beaches are rocky, the views are breathtaking and the serenity of it all is another reason this day feels so right.

There is absolutely nothing about 'the old days' I shall miss. This day shows me that the new days will be more delightful in every way! I am sitting here with nothing but the warmest feelings in my heart, barely able to contain how good I feel. I feel like the world is opening up to so much more, and I am certain that you feel the same way too. This is just the beginning of something absolutely fantastic and beyond the scope of words. This is an extremely uplifting day!

That is why I chose to write this letter on the morning of your wedding. I wanted to accurately capture the emotions of this important day. Those emotions are overwhelming happiness and peace. I woke up this morning on very little sleep, yet feeling fantastic and so incredibly ready to begin a new chapter of life, and I'm sure you feel the same. Everything feels shiny and new.

I want nothing more than for you to be happy and what makes you happy is most often what makes the people around you happy. By making this day a reality you have brought much happiness, hope, and inspiration into the lives of others. I can't speak for everyone, but I know for a fact you have done that for me. You always have, and always will be, my inspiration, and this day is just more proof of that."

And with that, Connor gave me away, launching us both into our next stage of development.

With this marriage, I felt something inside calling me to change my last name to Blake's. I was in two minds about it. As a fifty-year-old woman who's name was synonymous with her work, it wasn't going to be easy. Then there was a sixteen-year-old girl inside who fondly remembered writing Mrs. Jonni Gray all over her diary pages all those years ago. Those things aside, I talked it over with Connor. It was one of those pivotal moments.

Although he resided on the planet for two more years, he and I both knew our worlds were changing now. We couldn't stay suspended, ageless, timeless, together forever. At least not on the earthly plane. We both longed for it, though, and communicated that longing with each other often. But we also felt deep inside that that wasn't what we signed up for in this lifetime.

If we had resisted our individual independence, if I hadn't married, if we hadn't moved apart, we would have regressed to a co-dependency state with all the repercussions that would have meant. For awhile, I tried to straddle two worlds - apparently it's a common theme in my life - travelling between my life as Blake's life partner, and my life as Connor's soul partner. I was being split in two and knew I was ready to crack. So I did.

Helping Connor move between apartments one afternoon, I unknowingly stepped into a cement stairwell and dislocated and broke my left shoulder. Connor raced down the flight of stairs to be by my side. I told him I was fine, just shaken, and asked him to help me get up. It was then that my body started registering the split. The last time I felt a pain like this was when my pelvis was widening, preparing me for childbirth. An interesting correlation now.

My shoulder was obviously out of its natural alignment. Instinctively, but mostly to ease Connor's worried look, I slowly, carefully popped the deformed broken shoulder back fully into its socket. Together, we painfully walked the five blocks to the nearby hospital where I asked Connor to phone Blake, who was several hours away.

In those waiting hours in the emergency room, Connor and I talked and communed deeply. We both sensed the message my body was taking on. It was loud and clear, and at the same time massively painful. It reflected a perfect metaphor, as our bodies so often do. I told him gently, lovingly, that I didn't know how to do both worlds anymore. It was breaking me. Literally. I said I could feel the soul promise and the human resistance. Connor agreed that he felt it as well. Neither of us knew what to do about it though.

Connor's remaining year on the planet was all about stretching our ability to have the same soulful connection while not being physically together. It was practice made perfect. We could feel the promise to be energetically inseparable and that promise never faded. It was heightened. We practiced living our lives as we kept the love bond strong. Each of us could feel the glory of the other and the consistency of it was uncanny.

Every so often, I would lose the connection, like dropping a phone line, distracted by my physical realties. Connor would tell me later he felt those times as energetic abandonment. He knew I was always there and always loving him, but he was not feeling it energetically strong. He would be right, of course, and I would refocus and reposition my love connection with him. Day in and day out, morning and night, we expanded our energetic fields to include each other at all times. When he lost the plot, I would share that with him. We had built up such a clear and open communication style over the years that these conversations were easy and always loving.

I would compare the process to being present or distracted when you were with someone. You can either be deeply engaged with them, or thinking of something else. You can even be somewhere neutral in between. Connor and I organically, magnetically, were always deeply attuned and engaged with each other when we were physically together. The trick now was to have the same depth of engagement - because we longed for it - without the physical attachment.

But even as Connor and I practiced consistent non-physical engagement, neither of us saw this as preparation for his inevitable departure. It's only in hindsight that it all makes sense.

A few months later, he felt compelled to spend an entire weekend with me lovingly sorting out all the boxes, albums, and memory cards of photographs we had accumulated over our time together. He painstakingly scanned and labeled countless photos, compiling them in iPhoto digital library files, keeping one copy for himself and blue toothing another copy to me. He needed to complete this task, working long into the nights to do so. Once our digital photo files were finally complete, and equally shared, Connor exhaled, satisfied.

That Christmas (our last) I too felt the need to create something to signify our story and the end of this chapter. From the collection of photos Connor had compiled for us, I selected one from each of the thirteen vehicles he had painstakingly bought, fixed up, and drove in his life - including a boat! Then I created a simple photo memory book, believing he needed to embrace his courageous, adventuresome spirit in all its glory. He was planning a solo motorcycle holiday down the coast of the United States for that summer. I made sure every one of his vehicles, including the motorcycle he would drive down the coast, was in the book.

Other loved ones were leaving ahead of Connor. The energy of closure was apparent. Connor's grandmother, his father's mother, chose to cross over at the amazing age of 100. Connor and she had been very close, and he felt her passing deeply, carefully, thoughtfully. Then, within months, my mother, his other grandmother, exited. I had been expecting it for years, and it felt like a chapter of my past was now finally over. The end of an era. Ever beside me, Connor and I talked about the significance of these women in our lives. I could feel Connor's strong, soulful connection to these life-changing events.

As difficult as it was - and it was - we both felt the importance of playing the expected human roles we chose in this life. A mother and son do not carry on an exclusive intimacy past the natural, chronological stages of independence. Connor had his girlfriends, with all the heartbreaks and joys that go along with them. He had his passions, his causes, and his friends. He had his college days and his Saturday night band practice. He had his own apartments and cars and motorcycles. We appeared normal in that regard, even though we prioritized each other. To that extent we felt as though we had accomplished all that we needed to do together.

It was in that vein that Connor started dropping O'Connor from his name, trying it out at first, and then legally changing it. His middle name was Jordon, so he became known simply as Connor Jordon, a man of his own identity. Both of us could feel the separation happening; this was just part of the process.

We had reached the peak of intimacy in physical form. Life was changing, and would never quite be the same again. We had had our time in the sun.

CHAPTER NINE

SHADOWS

I'VE ALWAYS HAD AN OVERWHELMING fear of being out of control in a car. Panic attack fear.

I was in a handful of car accidents as a child and still have all the scars to prove it. Once, while on a family outing one afternoon, we actually drove into a house. But that's not what the fear is all about. I waited until I was twenty-seven years old to get my driver's license. I calculated that waiting eleven years longer than everyone else might buy me a bit of time to relax the fear. But it didn't.

Once I started driving, the first car accident I had was when I was eight and a half months pregnant with Connor. Black ice. Late evening. Snowing. Once my white Honda Civic hit the black ice, it slipped sideways down a steep, snowy ravine until it met with the bottom. The muddy ravine water began seeping into the cracked-open passenger-side window. My huge belly was firmly pressed against the gear shift, and my seatbelt was contracted. I wasn't going anywhere. When I finally looked up toward the road, I could make out a chain of hand-holding souls heading down the embankment toward me. Drivers of cars that had seen the accident slowed down to a stop. They formed a human rope as they cautiously made their way down to my sideways vehicle. The door was jammed up against the side of the ravine, but they rocked my car back and forth to set it free. Someone smashed my seatbelt lock, and then several more people wrangled my very pregnant self out of the vehicle and up the slippery slope. The snow was falling harder, making this no small feat.

These were the days before cell phones were in every pocket. An ambulance arrived soon after - "by chance", the driver said - and I was taken to the emergency room. My husband had been called and was able to join me. My water had broken, and the doctor on call said my baby would need to be delivered within twenty-four hours.

Try as I might, I could not dilate enough to birth Connor. My body was still in car-accident shock, and it froze. I was induced again and again and again, and still nothing. Apparently I can be stubborn that way. Finally, after thirty-three hours of trying everything, an emergency C-section was performed and Connor came out healthy and vocal.

It would make sense that my fear of being out of control in a car never diminished after that. Instead though, it took a strange turn. I stopped being able to be a passenger in a vehicle. Prior to the car accident I could ride a bus or ride with a friend, although half the time my panic would get the better of me and I'd wind up bailing out of either vehicle. But still, more than half of the time I could make it work. But now, I couldn't.

I had no fear of driving myself, and I drove a lot. I had several more accidents over the years, even totalling my Saturn in one of them, but I never developed a fear of driving myself. My fear was only when I was being driven: the fear of being out of control and in a vehicle. I went to therapists of every kind. I did regressions, tapping, hypnosis. Nothing dialled down the fear, although a lot of other issues were successfully dealt with. In hindsight, it was because the therapist and I always assumed the fear was about the past. No one thought it was about the future.

In the meantime, I resigned myself to always being the driver and rarely being the passenger. There were times in life when that wasn't always possible, but I thought of it in the same way one would consider an allergy. I avoided it ninety-nine percent of the time and had a panic attack one percent of the time. It was the best I could do, and I got on with my life.

Over the years when my siblings began transitioning, I noted they died in car accidents. Each had lost control of their vehicle. My fear was definitely locked in.

When Connor turned sixteen and was eager to drive, I effortlessly taught him. We went on many exciting road trips, zig zagging around the continent to better his skills as a driver. I was never afraid when he drove and I was the passenger. Even when it was pitch-black, snowing, and Connor had to weave in and out of a convoy of semi's on an unfamiliar highway, I never felt the fear I normally felt. As long as Connor and I were both in the car - whether I was driving or he was - my fear wasn't present. If he was with me, I was fine. It was my only exception, and my only clue.

Connor loved to drive, and over the six years he had a driver's license, as I've said, he bought, fixed up, and sold, many vehicles. In hindsight, he tried to squeeze a lot of living into those six driving years. Each vehicle had a reason and purpose for buying and selling, and with each vehicle my fear of something happening to Connor increased. I always told him I trusted his skills as a driver, but it was the other drivers I felt were not paying attention. My senses were sharp and keen that something could happen to him that involved another driver, and I knew I was powerless to do anything about it.

A month before Connor transitioned, I drove us both to a ski resort town about a hundred kilometres away. The winding two-lane highway was a breeze, and we were both deep in conversation when I rounded a corner and Connor spotted a black yearling bear on the side of the mountain. As I glanced to the side to take a peek, the young bear chose to enter the roadway directly in line with my oncoming Volkswagen. I was in a wide turn and my visibility was impaired. A glance in my rear view and side mirrors gave me the information that a vehicle was coming up beside me and another one was on my tail. I could do nothing but take my foot off the gas and let the car collide with the bear.

As anyone who has ever hit an animal knows, swerving is a poor and unsafe choice to make. Still, it's the logical one, and one I would likely have made if I hadn't heard Blake's voice in my head. Ever the safe driver, he's told me tales over the years of other drivers hitting deer and even moose as the animals walked onto the roadway. He always finishes his stories with clear instruction on how I should proceed if the situation ever happened to me. I was programmed, and I responded accordingly.

Knowing we were going to have to hit the bear, Connor went into an emotional tailspin. I rarely recall seeing him so shaken. Pulling over the car and accessing the situation meant calling 911. After that we got out to check on the bear. He had been severely hit in the head and death would take him any minute. I reassured Connor that the bear felt nothing and was likely not even in his body anymore. Connor heard me, but the emotional trauma went deep.

Our car was still drivable, but the front and passenger side would need repair. Connor's emotions were the priority though, so once the police arrived and took over the situation, I drove him to the closest lunch spot I could find and we spent hours talking over his triggered fears. He tried his best to put it into words, but like my fear of being out of control in a car, his interpretations found nothing that really helped. This wasn't about the past. It was about the future.

It's evident now that Connor's soul was tidying things up. He drove his motorcycle to all the places he had loved growing up: towns, streets, apartment buildings, restaurants, schools. He would call me or text me each time and we'd share stories. "Remember when..." He worked round the clock to get a second motorcycle he was tinkering with, up and running, enough to present it to a female friend at her birthday party, the night before he left on his amazing journey, saying, "It's not quite finished yet, but I wanted you to see it and to know it's coming."

In Connor's final few weeks, he made an extra effort to spend quality time with specific people: friends from his past, ex-girlfriends, work mates he was close with, his father, and stepfather, Blake. They all saw him one last time as he left them all with deep, abiding, authentic and lasting love from his soul-centred self. I was the last person he connected with. He had his closure with everyone. And on some level, we all had ours.

When a vehicle struck Connor as he attempted to cross the street in a designated crosswalk, the damage to the driver's truck was the same damage my car had sustained when I hit the bear. There are huge differences, of course. Whether in a hurry, or distracted, or indifferent, the motorist who killed Connor ran a red light in a crosswalk. People are not wild-life. We have traffic lights for good reason. Still, it's what the two incidents have in common that draws my attention and gives me confirmation of the deeply emotional response Connor had to the bear.

Connor had always had huge, wide hands - 'bear paws,' we called them. Even as a young boy he would position one of his hands next to mine and exclaim with delight that his were already bigger. Giggling girls with Connor-crushes who worked at the same place he did all nicknamed him "cute bear". And he was always known for his exceptional 'bear hugs'. Connor's were extra special and came right from his soul, and everyone knew it. I don't ever remember him waking up, or meeting me somewhere, or coming home, when he didn't walk up to me and give me the most affectionate bear hug of love. Those early years of our constant snuggles gave him his signature, and so Connor lovingly lavished his bear hugs of love on everyone.

Yes, bear had always been a theme for Connor. My mind connected the bear, the fear of losing control in the car, the fear of other drivers around him, into the tapestry of it all. When you find obvious signs, nothing seems random.

CHAPTER TEN

THE AFTERMATH

EACH MORNING I WOULD WAKE UP and for about four seconds the world wouldn't spin. For four precious seconds everything felt humanly safe. And then, like a tsunami, the three-dimensional reality would hit me and I'd sputter, choke, and drown again. Every single morning I felt Connor die again. And I started to age very quickly.

Looking back at it now, I would describe it as a horror version of the movie "Groundhog Day". And as much as the spiritual, intelligent side of me could grasp the soul-based meaning of it all, the devastation to the shattered nervous system went on and on. We are so often bound in this three-dimensional reality even though we sense or we know it's an illusion. Connor's passing was a firm reminder for me. It doesn't get any firmer.

My heart was caught in the middle of the two realities and was being pulled apart. I was adrift at sea with nothing to anchor myself to. I had lost the connection to physical Connor, and now

I was losing the initial connection I had had to non-physical Connor.

Planting myself in the human experience of it all was beyond painful, so I resisted. Sleep eluded me until the wee hours of the morning. Time held no meaning. I didn't want to see anyone. I didn't want to be here. But I kept working. I started with emailing those who would be most affected by this sudden turn of events.

"Beautiful ones, it devastates me to have to share this news with you, but our Connor was suddenly taken from us on Monday night in Salem, Oregon. This wasn't a bike accident. He made it through most of his incredible journey on motorcycle to Las Vegas and back - happy, healthy, and unscathed. I've attached the selfie he took just days ago and sent to me.

He had stopped in Salem for the night on his way home to Vancouver, and after texting me, decided to go for a walk to explore the area by foot until we were to FaceTime a few hours later. He was struck and killed in a crosswalk by a driver who ran a red light.

As the embodiment of love, he is in our hearts and spirit. There is meaning in everything and this too has a purpose. I will connect with you about death and loss at another time."

It was like putting a powerful magnifying glass over myself with a glaring spotlight and saying, "Watch. I will share my process as it happens, with you". I couldn't bear it, but I knew I had to.

When a parent dies it feels as though you lose your past, or at least a significant part of your past. When your child dies, and in this case, your only child, it feels as though you lose your future. I had no where to go, but within.

The multidimensional greater reality was giving me my only reprieve. As long as I was connected to that belief and experience I was floating more than I was walking. I was in silence more than I was weeping. I was working with clients and students with effortless skill. Anything that took me out of the here-and-now three-dimensional reality that said my only child was no longer here was welcome.

I wasn't distracting myself; I was no longer interested in being myself. The role in life I had most cherished was now completely null and void, and that identity with it. I no longer wanted to be part of the planet on these terms.

Everyone close to me would have understood if I had quietly wrapped up my life at that point. They all knew the soulful bond I shared with Connor. I had no fantasies or intentions of ending my life. That would have taken too much energy. But I welcomed no longer waking up in the morning. I never wanted to go to sleep, wake up, eat, or move my body again. I could never imagine being happy again. I longed to be with Connor in the realm I knew he existed in, and I knew I was a breath away from exiting. My husband, Blake, must have sensed I had a will to die or no longer had a will to live. Either way, he stayed very close, putting me on suicide watch. And rightly so.

Suicide is a denial of our spiritual identity. It's a denial of our life's purpose. But just because we don't remember our life's purpose and plan, doesn't mean life is meaningless. It's not that I wanted to die to end the misery of living. It was that I knew where Connor was. I knew that I couldn't get to where he was unless I went through my own transformation from physical to non-physical and I longed for that. From all the regression work

I have done over the years, I have deep memory of that space, that realm, that connection, and I felt I was somehow deprived of it now.

As a fully committed mother, I lead the way. I would go first and check to make sure it was okay before my child followed. But I couldn't now. I was being held back. In my stubborn, three-dimensional, innate mother identity, I felt savagely violated. Cut to the quick. Eliminated. That role was over in a heart beat. It's not as though I watched my only child endure a slow death, wringing out the pain and the process in equal tears. This was swift and blunt and seemingly senseless. I needed time to process it all.

I'm an internal processor. I connect dots and grasp meaning and only then look outside for soul-to-soul communication with another. For years the only person I could do that with was Connor, but of course Cheryl, my co-channeller, stepped in making those connections with me on that soul-to-soul wavelength now. We started talking every day. Connor's transition was something we both knew had greater significance to our purpose and promise in this lifetime. It had layers of meaning and choice, and those layers had to be unpeeled slowly.

We still only channelled Sage Council once a month or so, knowing it was more important than ever that I use my connection with Connor to strengthen my own understanding of it all. When we did channel together though they told me: *"You are one of the blessed few who knows your purpose and your work. You are one of the blessed few who knows that your work is infusing love in the people that you touch. And of course you want to escape because you know that space. You have strong memory of the freedom of that space. And now that Connor has joined that space, you feel that you will not be happy unless you are in that space.*

And we wish to tell you, Jonni: not yet.

Of course, as a human, any choice you make is within your power. We know the pain can feel so deep, so unending, and we are with you in every second of that feeling that you have.

When Mother Mary watched Jesus transitioning from Earth to Spirit, she remembered that he was on loan, that they had made an agreement in the spiritual realm, that she would be the honoured mother of his presence on the planet. And when he transitioned, she felt the pain that any mother would feel with the loss of a child, and she also had an instant remembering that this was what they agreed. You are *remembering, Jonni. You* are *remembering."*

I exhaled upon receiving that message, and went deeper, still.

I had loved Connor like no other. I had loved him as his spiritual essence. I had loved him on this journey of life. I had loved him to his exit, and beyond, but I couldn't do a funeral. I couldn't do a wake or even a celebration of life. I couldn't do a memorial service of any kind. Connor wasn't "dead". It wasn't over. It was just different now, so it would be untruthful if I took part in anything other than what I felt.

Then I noticed a huge double-trunked tree in our backyard that called me, and I knew that was where I would put Connor's ashes. Strange as it may sound, both Connor and I had talked about what we wanted to happen to our bodies after we were no longer on the planet. It was understandable to have conversations such as this. After all, he had been right beside me through all the family transitions that I was in charge of. I was the stronger human. I had buried each member of my family. I could do this, I thought. He would do the same for me. Connor simply wanted to be cremated.

I wrote an email to those whose hearts were in alignment with mine, to those who knew there was greater meaning than simply a loss, that, over time, one is suppose to get over.

"We are burying Connor's ashes this SONday at 9 AM in our backyard under our magnificent old soul CONifer tree. There is one very special tree on our two-and-a-half acres that is most prominent and stands alone and majestic amongst the grass and dandelions. About four feet up, the tree's trunk splits in two and both trunks grow equally tall and straight, side-by-side.

Connor always said he and I were from the same DNA code and so we'd be together forever. And even though he and I had two bodies in this lifetime, we were twins, connected at the heart and soul.

Please join us in an energetic group hug on that day and time and we will feel you and you will feel us. Connor and I always feel each other, even when we are not physically together."

Before Connor transitioned, I told him I felt as though we were twins. I said I bet there was a lifetime when we were. He agreed. We knew we had the parent child in reverse dynamic, and the feeling of being siblings, but this twin feeling always stuck with me. The internal message I received after Connor's transition was that although all souls expand out from the Source, Connor and I are the same soul divided in two *after* our original soul split from Source.

Think of it like this: all branches on a tree come off of the main trunk. Branches then come off those main branches. Those branches can be thought of as soul mates, sometimes. If they have romantic connections, we might call them twin flames. In this metaphor, think of twin souls as two buds on the tip of the branch that have almost the same spiritual DNA.

Connor and I have been together in almost every incarnation. Twin souls have a love connection that lasts through eternity. It's why the two of us stay so connected whether in physical or non-physical form, and why we continue to work together - he from where he is, and me from where I am. That's why we always understood each other at a soul level, so well. We are one soul divided so we can accomplish more in each cycle of incarnation. We are in two different dimensions trying to help change lives, including our own.

The days and nights were slipping by, merging and dividing into strange patterns. I had phenomenal connectivity with Connor just before falling asleep or upon waking up. When we rise above our grief, when we get out of our brain's insistence on the facts, there's a point of knowing the greater reality we can tune into. Connor couldn't become physical again, but I could become non-physical in my sleep and in my meditations. It was my only chance, I thought. Meditation was difficult, but not impossible. I fumbled my way through. The rest of the time I stumbled.

I had every important and significant book on my bookshelves to help me through the stumbling. But I didn't want them. Not yet. (I would consume them months later) I stubbornly just wanted Connor, and nothing else would do. Reading books felt like work, and my relationship with Connor was never work. So I struggled, stuck.

I didn't have the consistency or ability to be either in constant grief, or constant spiritual connection. I was straddling two worlds, yet I wasn't fully in either. I was in no-man's land and Connor wasn't there to model what to do. Instead, he was there to energetically inspire. And every so often I would get a nudge of influence, as small breadcrumbs started to appear. Again.

The house Blake and I had moved into two days before Connor transitioned had been neglected for years. That was one of the main reasons why we bought it. It needed a lot of love, yet it was that exact ingredient I felt I no longer had. Still, ever sensitive to my environment, I could feel the walls mocking me. The last owners had decided to brighten the place up by painting every wall either fluorescent orange, lemon, lime, or strawberry. I felt the sorbet-coloured pallet mocking me like a sarcastic joke. I had to do something about it. The love-pie was long gone, and the only other hint of a breadcrumb that Connor knew would get me moving again was to alter my environment. Over the years, Connor and I painted all twenty of those homes and offices. Truthfully, he watched more than he painted, but our conversations and laughter would keep me going.

Then I remembered Connor polishing everything he could get his hands on in kindergarten to re-establish order after the loss of a loved one. I got the message and started rolling out neutral colours onto the animated walls. I told myself, "just one wall a day." And every day I felt my environment calm down. It was a necessary reflection.

Our new home was on acreage, so if I wanted to I could be in absolute isolation and lose my physical bearings in the act. As emotionally unanchored as I was though, I knew I needed to ground myself in the Earth. The first walk was painful. I walked around our property, stroking every tree, touching every plant, rubbing the leaves between my thumb and finger, desperately trying to feel something. I went through the motions, but I was numb. How could I ever expect to connect with non-physical Connor when I couldn't even appreciate nature?

Sessions with Sage Council would yield more direction: *"We are asking you to expand your capacity to love. When you are ready, we want you to love being on the planet. When you are ready, we want you to love every experience that you've had to have as a human in this existence. When you are ready, we want you to love that you've been given a gift in your work to help heal others and to move the planet forward."*

It felt like an impossibly tall order, but as always, I started with my work, for it was through my work that I felt the spiritual connection most. And through the spiritual connection I could feel Connor. When I stepped into my work, I could function. Because my heart felt extremely open and porous, I started caring more than I had ever cared before. Everyone went through a litmus paper test of authenticity and my caring depth calibrated to match. I had no control over it. It was uncanny. Friends, clients, and everyone in-between were either on my heart-based frequency, or not. I felt it and acted accordingly. I know I cut out a lot of people from my life. At first it was the need to be alone and the preservation of energy, but later I realized it was simply a refined focus my life was taking on. I didn't seem to have a say in it for it cut to the bone of being authentic. Repurposed.

After each conversation with Cheryl, and Sage Council, I was noticeably clearer and lighter. I was connecting dots rapidly, confirming the threads that I could now see were all woven together. I could feel the truth on a cellular level. Information, confirmation, mental and emotional processing. Then more information, more confirmation, more mental and emotional processing. I would smile one minute and weep the next, and that was the process of integration. It felt as though I was having the original birthing contractions again, but so much worse.

The grief when a mother loses a child is said to be one of the worst emotional pains there is. It's more than cutting off your arm. It's cutting out your heart but keeping you still alive. The feeling that my only child, my soulmate, my twin, was gone, was beyond excruciating. And persisting in me was the stubborn *human* feeling that I had lost him.

I knew it was an illusion. I really did know better, but that's why I was harder on myself than I needed to be. The illusion can appear quite real in the emotional system, even though the mind is aware of so much more. And I knew the only way to move through that illusion and integrate it into my knowingness was to understand Connor's choice to be birthed and his choice to exit.

I had done the work with so many clients before him. And over the years I recalled the grieving parents who had come to see me, having lost their children in accidents. They needed to understand why. What had I said to those parents? How had the greater reality perspective helped them? I needed to apply what I knew, to work it through.

CHAPTER ELEVEN

UNDERSTANDING CONNOR'S CHOICE

THE ONLY WAY THROUGH THE PAIN I was in was through working. And working meant sharing. I couldn't neglect the promise I made to serve. Just as Connor had always modelled to me, it was necessary for me to model for others. As absolutely private a matter as this was, as completely vulnerable as I was, I had to step outside of my little bubble. People wanted me to.

Over the next few months, I wrote a handful of significant blog posts as teaching/sharing opportunities. I talked about why we choose to exit when we do, the meaning of life and death, and the greater reality always at play.

Still, people wanted to know more. They wanted to know specifically. They were hungry, but they were also respectful and gentle. I was more than grateful. My inner most private world was becoming all mixed up with my public identity. Worlds and realities felt as though they were colliding, yet I knew they were melding together. One can't straddle forever.

Privately, I was connecting dots. I couldn't help it. My mind works in images more than anything else and I was seeing things connect like a matching card game. With every two things that lined up, the revelation would cause me to pause and integrate the truth. I had been processing my mother's passing just four months before Connor's, and, as she was the last of my former family members - for they all transitioned long before reaching old age - it was a monumental time of soul-centred reflection.

When that last card is played you're able to see what everyone had in their hands, and that was the case after my mother's exit. I saw how all the other players - father, siblings, grandparents - played their hands based on what they were dealt in this lifetime. It's a fascinating poker game, when all is said and done. The roles we choose in each and every lifetime take on much meaning and significance, especially when you see how they all interrelate.

So every day I looked at this extraordinary past of mine, with Connor's choice of exit as part of it all. Like a kaleidoscope that was turned once again, the mosaic reflection revealed even more imagery.

One day I became aware of the fact that my father had been twenty-nine years old when he lost his only son. When I was twenty-nine years old I conceived my only son. My father never got over the loss of his son, and even though he had four daughters, he became a heavy-hearted, depressed man, and would remain so for the rest of his life. As an emotional sponge I attempted to carry the pain my father, Jonny, carried in his heart and lungs. But there was nothing I could do. He was lost to us all. It was no surprise to me, therefore, that I unconsciously chose to bring a male child into the world for my father. Connor was his only grandson. When my father transitioned, Connor was five years old. I was five years old when my father's only son passed on. It doesn't fit together more perfectly than that.

The connections between each of the family members started falling into place in rapid succession. Why they chose to be born into this family, why they exited when they did, how each of their choices affected the whole, and how Connor's birth, purpose, and transition was pivotal in it all. Like I said, an ever-turning kaleidoscope.

In previous years when I'd had the continued misfortune to keep losing family members, I shared those experiences and the greater meaning behind them, as blog posts. People who had lost loved ones, people who had lost siblings, people who wanted to work with someone who shared their belief system about life, death, and afterlife, came out of the woodwork. I felt the promise I had made to the 'sharing your process' role I was to play in this lifetime.

Those I worked with were used to seeing me as a teacher of the non-physical and spiritual reality, yet my private stories spoke beyond theory and practice. Experiences create the real substance, and the synchronicity of it all was not lost on me. I was set up to be at this place, at this time, with these people. That, I was certain of. I knew that somewhere deep inside someone called out, "And... Action", and I was on cue, hitting my marks, speaking the truth of my lines.

After people ask how, and when, and where, they pause. Then they ask why. At least that was my experience after people found out about Connor's passing. The people who asked me why were asking the question to affirm their belief that there's order in the universe. Their human experience says that this is out of order. Children don't die before parents. Spiritually aware young adults with much to contribute to the planet do not transition off the planet when there is still so much potential to be realized.

Yes they do. And yes, there is order in the universe.

Prior to incarnating on the Earth, we create a series of possible exit points - times when we may choose to leave the planet. Your soul chooses for your human. Your human is frightened of the unknown. Your soul knows.

Having conducted tens of thousands of past-life regressions in my career, I have walked people through countless exit points in their lifetimes. One of the questions I almost always ask their spirit, after they've exited their physical body, is, "Why did you choose to leave that life at that particular time and in that particular way?" Their spirit always provides a clean, clear, meaningful answer. Nothing is random.

I can summarize those answers into two distinct reasons. The spirit of the person either sees no possibility of realizing their potential - their soul's mission - under the current situation, and so opts to exit, or quite the opposite: they accomplish their soul's contract and choose to return to their full non-physical experience.

I'm making it sound simple, but for the soul who is making the choice, it is. The soul knows there is so much more than the human experience, so much more than meets the eye, or even the 'I'. It knows why they incarnated and why they need to evaluate that choice at given times. But the human experience can be very, very different. And difficult. The human perspective is so limited, so physical, and so finite. To ask your human to expand beyond those limitations is asking a lot. It's the biggest stretch we ever have to make, but unless it's made, we continue to be in pain or suffering or denial, or ignorance.

So how does one make the stretch? How can we connect the dots between what our soul is doing and choosing, and what our human is experiencing?

From my vantage point I know that by connecting to that soulful realm on a daily basis we stretch, strengthen, and reinforce the connectivity between our human and our soul. I have been doing that for as long as I can remember. Adversity originally sent me there, but the pleasure and connection keep me there. Meditation answers my questions, satisfies my human needs, and gives me a reason to live.

I know this entire human experience is temporary, a smaller reality within a greater reality, and I'm not one to pretend or choose denial. Sooner or later, those choices create too much suffering. The empowered choice is to keep that connection going, deepening it, expanding into it, using it as the power source and the memory source. Then it serves me well when the human that I sometimes feel like asks "why". It answers "why". It illuminates "why". It satisfies my human side enough that she can go on.

Sage Council later expanded on Connor's choice of exits for me. I always valued the confirmation of my remembering self. *"Connor chose this point of exit. There are multiple points of exit for every human being. Connor longed to expand his heart to even higher capacity than he had in his physical form. Transitioning behind the veil of illusion and joining us on this side of energy and love allows him to be his most expansive self. He is free, formless love. Connor wants you to know that he is with us. He was instantly with the energetics of Sage Council at his point of exit. We are part of the family that greeted and held him, and continue to be so.*

When most people pass rapidly, there is a time of confusion between the physical exit and the integration into spirit and energy. Connor made the journey extremely quickly, as he was already connected to his energetic self. He rapidly moved from point of exit to integration into spirit and energy. We see blue and gold and white lights around him now. He is so expansive. Feel his energy integrate with yours now, Jonni. He is sending you waves and waves and waves and waves of love.

Connor made the promise to come into this lifetime and to allow you full independence once you and he had achieved a certain level of intimacy. Your role in this lifetime is independent planetary service. Connor was here to support you, and he did that.

He also knew that if he exited at the time that he did, he could support you and help you at a much greater level as your spirit guide. By removing the physicality of his essence, he could allow you, and give you, the gift of independence in this lifetime.

Connor's decision was to support you in your spiritual evolution. He came into this lifetime as a gift for he did not have to incarnate with you at this time. When planning his future, he chose with full heart to come in and support you, in your work, in your dharma, and out of his deep love and soul-connection for you.

We wish to tell you that this point of exit for Connor was the most divine gift - a love gift. He chose this exit point because he was complete with his freedom and exploration on the planet, and he wanted to go home in order to be truly free and to explore at the spiritual level. He knew that if he left at this time you would be able to move to your next level of expansion in your planetary work. He also knew that because of who you are, you would be able to sustain the connection to him in spirit form."

CHAPTER TWELVE

SHARING CONNOR

YES, CONNOR KNEW I WOULD BE able to *"sustain the connection to him in spirit form,"* for several reasons. First, our soul-based physical relationship prepared me for it. But equal to that, since 1996 I had grown to feel Sage Council's presence, their communication, and their love, and they have only been non-physical for me in this lifetime. I was practiced and primed to feel Connor's presence, communication, and love, therefore, when he was non-physical as well. My connection with Connor in the *physical* realm, combined with my communication with Sage Council in the *energetic* realm, meant that through all that love, I could connect with the vibrational ray that was Connor. How could I not?

Working and connecting with others kept opening up more understandings as well. As others asked questions, I found answers were simply given to me. As they made observations, I would smile and know. I could feel myself - hear myself

- speaking the wisdom that I knew was coming from those I love in the non-physical realm.

At first people wanted to know about life, death, the afterlife, choice, and why. As much as I was willing to share and engage with these conversations, I knew the greater story was about eternal love, and how that sacred love can be expressed and experienced as a soul-to-soul relationship in physical and non-physical form. But I had to answer their immediate questions first.

Many were using the story of life and transition and afterlife as a place from which to relate. A client wrote: *"Jonni, I was amazed by your response to your son's death, that you were grateful to have been his mother in this lifetime. Wow! I thought, of course, it is our soul's experience as a human in this life, but when the emotions of the human are so intense (as in losing someone so precious in your life), it's very difficult to remember the bigger picture. You spoke this truth the next day after this happened! I think I would have eventually gotten there, but not nearly so fast. Perhaps it is the meditation that you mention that helped you get there faster. I am so grateful to have you in my sphere of experience."*

The daily connection to soul through meditation is vital. Connor and I connected there by meditating separately and together, by loving together, communing together. It formed the necessary foundation that would take us through life and beyond. It definitely enabled me to process and integrate the transition much faster and deeper than most people, so I could model it as a choice for others.

There were others connected with my work who believed in the afterlife and the continuation of it all. They believed in both the three-dimensional reality and the greater reality and found the threads that joined the two. I was so proud of them for expressing publicly what is rarely talked about.

"A couple of days after Connor passed I was meditating and felt a tremendous urge to call out his name, so I did. He responded right away with "yeah", like he had been waiting. I almost chuckled. I said one word: "Why?" He answered back with, "For you, it's the knowledge that everything can change in a split second". I started to cry and he was gone. The phrase he spoke has been with me every second of every day since then. In the days and weeks leading up to this meditation, I had been stuck in a place of wishing my life was different - no kids, no husband - but Connor's words jolted me out of it pretty fast..."

Connor the conduit was working closely with me still. Showing up in dreams and meditations for others, instead of physically in groups and behind the scenes, now.

Over time, those people I connect with in my work turned the corner on their questions. Like my kaleidoscope, they saw something else that was awe-inspiring. They saw the love story, the soul-to-soul relationship that had been so present in physical form. They saw what that looked like, and they acknowledged it. I felt myself relieved. The soul-to-soul love was alive and well and was still working its magic.

"An intense and inseparable bond is not something you see and feel very often. What a pleasure it is to have experienced this connection with no limitations for us all to view."

"Images of Connor keep flashing through my mind. He always struck me as being an exceptional person. He was always smiling, open, warm, ready for anything, but most of all kind and so present. Not your typical teenage boy, ever. He struck me as

wise and mature beyond his years. More than anything though, I remember being struck by the connection the two of you had. I remember him coming in and picking you up after your classes. Your greetings were always so warm and full of respect and love. You seemed to be best friends, not mother and son. I thought the world would be a much better place if more parents and children had connections like yours. He had an incredible mother in you. I could feel how much you loved him when you were with him, when you talked about him, when he was around..."

During times of transitions, we can all meet at the crossroads of our heart-based realities. I told everyone that Connor was deeply integrated within my fibre and that we would continue to be together, just in different forms. As much as it was my privilege to be his mother for twenty-two years, ours was an other-worldly bond, and that is never broken. I told them that Connor was still my best friend, my twin soul, my champion, and greatest teacher. I would not be who I am without him. I explained that we have the most intimate and amazing bond, and that he is my spirit guide now. I let them all know that the lifetime we just shared had been a tremendous gift.

Even though I birthed Connor into this lifetime, even though my role was mother, I knew that Connor wasn't just mine. I never felt the significance of that as much as after his passing, though. He belonged to so many others, those he touched, those he modelled for, those who knew there was something more. They needed to share in the great love connection as well.

On and on the letters, emails, cards, and notes poured in, dozens and dozens and dozens, and always from people who knew either him or both of us. It kept reminding me that Connor and I had shared ourselves individually and together with the world without even knowing it, and that the sharing had to continue. Each opportunity was a teaching/sharing moment.

One of Connor's past school teachers wrote, "*...I wish I could share with you the love for Connor that I have been hearing from his friends, their memories and gratitude and laughter among tears. Their stories are about his enthusiasm and acceptance, about generous collaborations and endless creativity. They talk about music and cars and writing stories, and those times that only they know of when he was the one that listened, or the one that helped them see past a hurdle, or wrote a song that made them laugh. Mostly his fellow students are talking about the incredible friend he was and what that friendship has meant to them. They say it in different ways, but they each say that he was more comfortable being himself than anyone else they ever knew, and that he was their best friend. Every one of them say that. I feel so lucky to have shared Connor's company in those years, and in the years since. He was so kind and thoughtful and funny, his observations about the world were uniquely his own and he shared them with compassion. There is a place in my life that is his...*"

Yes, Connor was a friend to all, for his platform for friendship was always soul-based. He wouldn't have it any other way. It was the only way he and I could have a relationship as well. Anything less would have been a waste, would have diluted the pure love, reducing us from soul-to-soul, to role-to-role. I told those who wrote me that although Connor was no longer in physical form, his indomitable spirit lives on, and it's so much more than memory.

We were all blessed to have had him on our journey in life, to model for us what soul-based love looks like. One of Connor's friends said, "*I'm sure you will get a flood of emails telling you just how amazing your son is, for he has touched and enriched every life I know with his unique light. He had such a magnetic personality. He changed my life by being in it and making it that much brighter.*"

Another friend echoed, "*Connor truly was a magnificent human being. I consider myself so fortunate to have known him. We spent so much time together growing up that I know I wouldn't be the same person without having him in my life. Time never seemed to pass with Connor. Everything always was a constant. He always kept an open mind and an open heart. I have searched for that kind of peace of mind for so long. I can only hope to learn to be more like him.*"

Many people saw Connor as I did, through the lens of love. It opened up their hearts and sense of possibilities, inspiring them now more than ever. They told me: "*Connor had a fresh, youthful wonder about the world, yet he was also a true gentleman, unknowingly wise beyond his years. You raised an incredible human being. I feel his spirit will be with everyone his soul has touched. I sense his piercing blue eyes in the blue sky, his insatiable laughter in the wind, his love in all in our hearts. Connor is one of the most beautiful souls I will ever know.*"

I reminded them all that Connor was communicating with them too, and he was still very much here. I told them that we can feel him in the energy of our hearts, reminding them that it's not just memories. It's much bigger than that. Sometimes we almost hear him, or we believe we know what he would say. That's real communication. I told them to treasure it. His essence vibrates in our knowingness and we feel the connection.

In our three-dimensional ways, in our limited human body, that's almost as good as it gets. But it's far better to be multidimensional in order to connect with more. That's the way of the artist, the poet, the spiritual seeker, the creative...those who see and sense more than linear, logical order.

Connor, in physical form, was multidimensional. He's still in this world, just without the body. There are others like him. But no one ever replaces him. They are each very unique and spectacular.

I told them they could connect with Connor even more vibrantly when they were in multidimensional experiences and platforms such as dreams, meditations, music, nature, emotion. I reminded them that soul love connected them to him, and him to them. The rest was setting the stage for feeling it more. I reminded them that the rest of the world - the jobs, the commercialism, the routines - would all feel three-dimensional only for awhile, because that's how they so often exist: flat and numb to the heightened multidimensional senses that are craving more of the real, more of the multidimensional, more of the more.

Most people exist in that 'numb'. They seek out better jobs or money or people or things to fill that void, but that void isn't 'fillable' by those things. They seek to get, instead of seeking to give. Our multidimensional spirit wants to live purely and authentically in the energy of much, much more. It knows when it's feeling it. We feel it as love; we feel it as real.

For me, there were bad days and good, bad moments and good. The contractions still took over sometimes, and my knees would buckle and I would collapse in sobs. And there were times when the big love made my heart feel as though it would explode. And then there were moments, often in the middle of the night, or when I was walking in nature, when I was calm and quiet and I could feel the gentle waves of Connor's presence in my visceral body. It was all part of the integration. The recognition that he's still so here.

The trick was to allow him to be more than the physical body. Staring at pictures of his physical presence told my brain that he was gone. I struggled with that falseness. His physical body was gone, but he was not. Connecting to him without pictures and images allowed me to be with him as he is now - in all his glory. Then it was a matter of boosting or upgrading that Connor into my reality, instead of limiting him to being the Connor in physical-form only. It's a continual process, even though I know he's with me constantly: big and beautiful and loving. When I connect with him in that way, rather than just the memory, I feel him as my companion day by day. I feel him as my ever-present spirit guide.

Connor's purpose in my life was, and is, understood. Helping others to understand his purpose in their lives gives them completion, and allows them to reach the next level. There was one more person I knew could use that extra understanding. I felt the strongest pull to write a final letter to Connor's father, to state with clarity, the soul's promises. It was received in grace.

"We both had a purpose in Connor's life. Part of our purpose was to bring through, together, the loving soul that Connor was. And as we moved through life, and when the evolution of our

choices as individuals was to separate and no longer be together, that meant Connor, as a soul who was independent, chose to live with his mother, and I chose the role to guide and help this soul along on the planet. I took that role very responsibly and very seriously, every day. And I took it to my heart. Every decision that was made was for Connor's well being, and as the parent who knew the soul development he needed, what happened was perfect for the evolution of Connor.

The three of us had a spiritual agreement. I know my part of the agreement and I fulfilled my part of the agreement. And I know your part of the agreement, and you fulfilled yours as a father-figure to him, so that in the end he had more of a relationship with you as an adult than he did as a child.

The gift to you is that for the rest of your life, you get to remember that you had that relationship with Connor before he transitioned."

CHAPTER THIRTEEN

MESSAGES, PROMISES, GIFTS

IMMEDIATELY AFTER CONNOR WAS born I received two powerfully strong inner messages. One told me to be the very best mother I could possibly be. This was less a goal and more a deep promise I felt I had made to myself, and to Connor, before I came onto the planet. Even before I knew of things like "pre-incarnate state", the feeling that I had made that commitment was paramount. It was encoded so deep within that it was *the* priority above all else. I also knew I had to make every moment count. I had to create memories to last a lifetime. I had to give raising him and staying absolutely connected to him, my full attention, and connect deeper than I had ever done to anything or anyone before. This I felt was the promise: to stay connected and in communion with Connor through every stage of his life.

A month after Connor's transition, Sage Council confirmed the message for me, saying: *"Connor was an extremely fragile soul in human form. In spirit form he is powerful beyond belief. In fact, he is more expansive and happy in spiritual form than he ever was in physical form. The reason for this is because he was not of the earthly energy. He is, and was, a very highly evolved old soul.*

Your gift, Jonni, was that you were the perfect person to tenderly care for his alien soul while he was on the planet. You were able to protect his essence. Had he been with any other parental choice, he would have been squashed through the requirement to conform. He would not have been the joyful, creative, spontaneous boy and man that he was. Your gift was near unconditional love, and through you, he learned to trust in his connection to Spirit and to trust in his own power."

I cannot tell you how long I wept as those words filled my heart with teary honour at the opportunity I was given to care for his soul in this incarnation. Connor was, and is, the love of my life. In communication with him through Sage Council, he has said the same words to me.

"We say that time is compressed, and in very short time, Jonni, you have healed many, many lifetimes and unfinished agreements between you and Connor. Connor wants you to know that you are the love of his life and it is impossible for him to ever be apart from you. And through this agreement, he is now immortal, and through his immortality he can stay connected to you forever."

As much as caring for Connor in physical form was of utmost importance, how could I have ever known that the care was related to his transition to non-physical as well? It was only after his exit that I started recognizing another layer of that importance. How else could he have laid down the imprints of our immortal relationship in this focused life? By soulfully bonding with him in quantity and quality of time and space, we reinforced the next level of conduit energy. The next mission in our purpose had a foundation and platform from which to build.

The second powerful message that vibrated my very being after Connor was born was about the work I am currently in. I remember I tried to get very clear with exactly what I felt pulsating in my heart. Everything was changing and I could feel it. It wasn't just about having a baby. It was as if a whole new world was opening up, one that was far bigger than what I had currently been living in. It was a far bigger world than I could ever imagine.

The essence of Connor was connected to something. I could feel it. "What is it?" I pleaded in my journals. When I read back over them now, they are filled with the angst I had in attempting to describe the feeling. I wrote that I had to do the kind of work that modelled to Connor all we could be on the planet today. I had to make him proud of me and proud of us. I had to show him that I knew or understood what it was all about. Whatever the work was, it had to be soul-driven and I had to pour every ounce of trust into it.

Of course this didn't make a lot of sense to me at the time. I was in publishing and felt happy and secure. Why I felt I had to leave that industry and move in a different direction wasn't clear to me. The message, however, was so strong I had to pay attention. Even though I was offered a publishing contract worth three times the pay and would significantly elevate my status, I felt compelled to say no.

I knew I couldn't put Connor in daycare or even hire a nanny. I remember the almost panicky feeling I had that made those options non-negotiable. How could I leave him? It wasn't as though he was weak, colic aside. It was exactly the opposite.

He was so powerful and connected that when he looked at me he reflected my own power and connection - a power and connection only his presence made me aware of. It was a power and connection I needed years to cultivate and confirm. How could I put him in the care of others and get on with my life? That didn't make sense. I simply couldn't.

As the early years went by, the breadcrumbs Connor dropped, the seeds he planted in the books and the conversations and the questions he would ask me, led me to walk down this particular path of soul service that continues to expand and develop as I do.

Connor became a part of every aspect of my work, from those early days of planting surprise gifts in my home office, to being the greeter at the door to everyone who entered my office. I never dragged him to work. He insisted on being there, more often preferring it to hanging out with friends after school. Every client knew him. He chatted with all those who were open to it, and at the end of my work day he would ask me about every little detail of everything I did, everything I experienced, said, heard, felt - everything that happened on that day. I knew I should be asking *him* those same questions about his day, though. I accepted his modelling and did. But he started it. He led and modelled how to be a respectful, caring, connected, love-filled, soul-based human being.

Connor was always part of the background, watching, participating, on every level. It wasn't like a single-mom bringing her child to work. I watched him come forward or fade into the woodwork depending on the needs and desires of each client or participant. It was a graceful manoeuvre, and one that allowed him full access and connection, even as a master observer. Connor ran every errand, filed every report, picked out and arranged everything from flowers to furniture. His presence and energy consciously filled every corner.

Connor and I would walk together most evenings, zigzagging our way through urban Vancouver streets. The conversations were always elevated. Whatever was going on in our world or in our life, we would give it our highest perspective viewpoint and speak about it together. The subjects changed but giving them the greater perspective never did. We gave angst, meaning. We gave uncertainties possibilities. We gave creativity energy an outlet. This was most helpful in the creation of the work that most people saw as 'my work', but was really 'our work'.

Every idea, title, program, writing piece, choice, creation, all went through both of us. I know I could not have done it alone. We were most certainly in it together.

When he was eight years old, Connor created a gift certificate for me for my birthday. It was for $27 worth of web design work. He was thrilled to give it me. He wanted me to keep creating, and he fully supported it at every single level. And even though Connor was a boy and then a man in chronological measurements, he was/is my life partner, my creation partner, my business partner.

As Connor grew older I knew he could do certain things even if he had not yet developed the skill. I was turning the tables on him now, seeing in him the potential that he had always seen in me. And because of that, he created all the meditation music I used week after week, month after month, in my meditation groups. He created the magnificent sounds I used in my past-life regression sessions. He developed the look and functionality of my websites and social media. He took the photographs I would use in all my marketing. Other times he willingly modelled for photo shoots when I needed to capture participants. He created the marketing campaigns from ideas that mysteriously came out of him. I was always delighted and surprised. He was eager to help me realize them.

But far more significant than all that, Connor provided a specific energy in physical form in my trainings, meditation groups, workshops, lectures, and other gatherings. The impact of his presence in my work was to infuse the energy of our soul-to-soul partnership. In that vein, he planted himself, and was invited into the dreams and meditations of those I continue to work with. When I help others in my work, I am connected. That process connects me, allows me to connect to Connor, and carries on the pathway of conduit. I am on purpose then. It's the reason I am here, as Sage Council confirmed for me after Connor's transition.

"Connor's purpose was to come in at a time when you were choosing your vocation. His primary gift was to give you the job that you do and that you are here to do. His secondary gift was to be with you as you developed the skills and the gifts that you have in this lifetime.

We see the next evolution of the commitment of soul promise between you and Connor with the development of your ability to access Connor in the spiritual reality and in the other realms. Jonni, you will recall that when you would talk with Connor on the phone there was the frequency of voice-to-voice. That is a frequency used on the planet Earth, which communicates energetics and fields of expression, and specifically between soul groups and soul connections and soulmates. The connection you would get with the verbal frequency would give you that sense of solidity and connection to Connor as a human entity on the planet with you.

The earth field has a container of frequency, which is why when people talk of intuition or tuning in, they're close to it. It's the Earth's frequency that allows them, and you, to pick up on things, just as a telephone line would let you tune into Connor's human energy when he was in human form and you could sense if he was happy or sad or in despair.

That sense of connection is what is no longer solid because Connor has transitioned to the finer frequencies of the other realm of the inter-dimensional reality. Connor says to you, Jonni, that from his viewpoint, from his vantage point, his connection to you is as strong or stronger than ever before, and that he is constantly, energetically whispering in your ear."

Yes, he whispers in my ear. He whispers the same love vibrations he always has. Connor reminds me: *"When I incarnated in this lifetime and chose you as my vessel, my mother, it was to complete the cycle of love that we have had for each other for centuries and centuries. You had served me in previous lifetimes but in this lifetime I feel it was me who served you, to cocoon you in love and security and support.*

It has been an honour to be with you on this lifetime journey, and I am not going anywhere. You will carry me with you energetically. I become part of your daily meditation connection. I speak to you while you are walking, working, meditating. I am now with you in essence, integrated into your cells, always with you as a remembering of <u>cherish</u>.

The emotion of love will keep us connected forever, and we do have future lives together. The future lives are to continue to expand planetary goodness. We are elevating the planet to such a level. This agreement, although painful for you in the physical, is extremely beneficial to planetary progress."

CHAPTER FOURTEEN

CHICKEN OR THE EGG

WHEN I LOOK AT THE BREATHTAKING soul-to-soul love story of Connor and I in one no-beginning-no-ending swoop using my own focused physical life as the point of view, this is what I see:

When I was a young girl, I lived inside myself. It was safe and rich and I didn't need anything else. I learned to go within for my needs. I would commune with nature, feeling the experience of myself reflected back in the majestic trees, the mountain paths, the open expansiveness of air, and the otherworldly element of water.

Throughout those years I had my companion energy and I communed with it daily. This energy was with me and through me. It wasn't like having an invisible friend. It was more than that.

This companion energy was both the most compassionate observer and was somehow also a part of me. Actually it didn't feel a part of me as much as more than me. Certainly more than the little Jonni that lived and breathed. This companion energy moved me in ways that felt extremely intimate and personal. Through it, I was seen for all that I was, and because of it, I was ultimately free. This companion energy was my best friend in the most non-physical way. Yet for an introverted young girl, it was a necessary reprieve.

People's teenage years, and their twenties, typically leave them bewildered and frustrated. The same was true for me as I was forced, like everyone else, to function and operate in the external world. I fumbled and stumbled and tumbled, again and again, trying to find my place in the world.

Throughout those turbulent years I continued to have this companion energy not just by my side but instilled within me. And even though it started to dim, as my external world needs took nearly all of my attention, I still felt as though we walked together, talked together, slept together, woke together. This energy companion never left me. It moulded itself around and through me, and strengthened me from within which is why I thought of it as an energy. I was never alone, even though to the outside world, I was most often alone.

Every time I stumbled and fell, my companion energy would pick me up and non-verbally reinforce my power and place within the cosmos. Nothing was exchanged, but I always knew I fit in the cosmos, in the greatness of it all. I got that. It was in physical life with other human beings that I was unsure, unknowing, and seemingly without common sense.

A month or so after my thirtieth birthday I had the car accident which resulted in my only child being born early. The trauma of the accident meant that all focus was on him and his needs. Colic set in for the first four months, but as the early years went by, little Connor became the constant glued-to-my-hips-and-heart companion. We walked together. We talked together. We slept together. We woke together. We shared almost everything and it was the most natural fit with another human being I have ever known.

Over the next few decades, everything in my life seemed to change. I was now on track, on purpose, in love, full of joy, courage, creativity, *externally* present and capable. Externally. That was something new. There was a confidence I was now able to translate from the greater reality to the physical reality. I always knew I had a place in the cosmos, but on the Earth? That was clearly questionable.

Now, year after year, with Connor's physical and soulful energetic presence, I slowly integrated those two realities so I could function on the Earth while staying connected to the greater cosmos. I had to. I was a single parent. But it was more than that. I had to because there was something about this mature soul in the young body that knew I could function better on the Earth than I did. He was the proverbial carrot on a string that would inspire me to do more for him than I would do for myself. To do more for us. And that was his purpose with me.

Together, he and I created work I adored. We found places to live that made us feel home. We earned good money and took holidays. We laughed and felt alive. I never even thought about my former energy companion. I had Connor now. He had me. We were twins in love, feeling intimate and personal.

And then... Another car accident, another early transition, and Connor was no longer in physical form, exiting the planet in the same way he had entered.

The human in me wept and wept, shattered at what appeared as a loss. After twenty-two years of having a solid, constant, physical, soul-based companion, I suddenly felt alone. Although this was the path I knew I had set up before I incarnated, it was a most delicate, vulnerable path. I was stumbling and fumbling and tumbling again. My human side was full of emotion at every turn - plummeting into darkness, and then suddenly overtaken with the biggest love I could expand to experience. But I couldn't stay in that imbalanced state.

Gradually, I started walking again, talking again, sleeping again, waking again. I stretched and stretched to reach more of the essence of Connor, the twin reflection I had known in solid form.

What I found was that Connor, in non-physical form, was no longer the young man I had birthed and grown up with, and that fact kept stalling me. I could connect with him like a memory, I could connect with him in my desire to share something with him, but those type of connections kept bringing me back to the physical reality that he was no longer here in physical form. And with that physical reality, I would plummet back down, disconnected and lost.

I was used to sharing every aspect of my processing perspective with him, and he with me, and I so wanted the Connor I knew to be able to discuss all this life-changing phenomena that was going on. It was *him* that had changed form and I wanted to discuss it with him. I could feel the irony of it and I was stuck. I was limiting my connection to Connor being only the Connor I had known in this incarnation. That was clearly not going to work. Yet the stubborn physical reality was that he was 'there' and I was 'here'. How was I ever going to connect the two up?

So I walked and I communed and when I wasn't plummeting in grief I picked up the breadcrumbs Connor was leaving and realized some significant facts. The first was that the largest part of me didn't buy into the fact that Connor was dead, that Connor was gone. I knew the physical facts were facts, but I didn't believe them. Not in my core. It did not resonate as truth. I didn't expect him to walk around the corner in physical form (although I longed for it), but it explained how I could still feel him all the time. He wasn't gone. It was more like he was invisible.

As a child, Connor's favourite book had been "Jimmy Takes Vanishing Lessons", by Walter Brooks. He asked me to read it again and again until he learned to read it himself. It's the simple story of a young boy living in a haunted house who's not fooled or frightened by the local ghost like everyone else. In fact, he outsmarts the ghost in exchange for vanishing lessons, so he too could appear and disappear at will. I remember that story now, and smile. Connor certainly took vanishing lessons well. A straight A student.

I think back to the day and time of the incident when Connor exited. We hear of so many people who seem to know when the transition of their loved one is about to happen. Their premonitions are immediate. I had none of those energetic, intuitive hits. In those early months after he transitioned, every time my mind would start to go to the scene of the accident, nothing happened. I drew a blank. I could not see or feel or experience in any way that event as a physical reality or even as an emotional black hole. The entire incident was simply neutralized for me, no matter how I snuck up on it. I never even dreamed of it. Something - someone? - was keeping me in the greater reality of it all.

Because I never felt Connor was gone, I sorely missed the physical and verbal aspects of our constant connection. The void was ever-present. Day by day, I kept searching the energetic galaxy for him, for that intimacy, but it was as though I couldn't find the correct frequency, the secret code. I had the occasional moment of connection and download, but it was like a static radio with only a few words spoken, and even those were often questionable.

But things started to shift when I began considering him in all his fullness. I had to respect the past mother/son relationship, but move on to the next chapter in our immortal love story.

I put away all photos of Connor, for the physical draw kept pulling me down like an addict needing a fix. Even though Sage Council was with me every step of the way, I was stubbornly holding onto my limited needs, ignoring the greater fact that Connor was so much more.

Now, in his non-physical essence, Connor was the being I had always felt he was, and as that being, he glowed with regal energy. I started referring to him as Connor 2.0, representing his graduation from one realm to the next. He liked that! It seemed I was catching on. He had much more to offer by shedding his 1.0 model. Now he could share his 2.0 with me. And with others.

Then one day, shortly after these realizations, I was walking and having a one-way verbal conversation with Connor 2.0, when it hit me all at once. It floored me. It stopped me in my tracks. My past, present, and future worlds suddenly, deliciously, and magnificently collided. I knew, with ever fibre of my being, that Connor 2.0 had been my companion energy all those years before.

I burst into tears of the grandest love. These were very different tears than I'd been crying over the preceding months. I want to tell you I paused and put the pieces together, but really it all added up in the flash of a lightening bolt. I knew. It was beyond logic, but I had the deepest sense of knowing.

The energy I was now coming to know (again) as Connor 2.0 had let me incarnate in this lifetime first, while he stayed energetically connected to me throughout those first thirty solitary years. As my energy companion, he provided me with the comfort and the intimacy necessary to thrive inside myself.

Then, thirty years later, I birthed him onto the planet to join me in physical form. How ironic that in my work I was guiding others to their soul connection and I birthed the very person who would be my soul guide. With the strength and solidness of our physical, energetic, and emotional connection, our mission was cemented on the planet.

Fast forward twenty-two years later and, at the best time for all concerned, Connor seemingly evaporated from solid form back into the ethers, joining me again as the companion energy he has always been, whether in physical form or not. This time, however, I wouldn't allow the connection to dim, or allow the external world to overwhelm it.

I stopped walking. I needed to take a breath. It was all so much. It was all so complete, yet my mind raced back over the last months wondering why it took me what felt like eternity to allow that old companion energy back in. Then I knew.

I stubbornly had only open been only to the essence of my son Connor in his limited capacity. Connor 2.0, however, was more than just my son now. I had to stretch and stretch, cracking open wider and bigger, until the energies all came together under the same vibration, with the same code, and the same connection: intimate, personal, loving and trusting. I'd recognize that energy anywhere.

CHAPTER FIFTEEN

THE EXPANSION

AS HUMAN BEINGS, WE GAIN SOME awareness and insight and then, unfortunately, we often forget it. It's not gone, but it's not as accessible as it once was, or needs to be, to be truly useful. As a consciousness expert, I know that this process is simply how we are built. It's not, however how we need to remain. We are evolving beings, and with focus and consistency we can gain awareness and insight, and consciously integrate it so it becomes part of our operating system. Installed. Upgraded.

When things seem to go sideways, when it feels as though you've been sucker punched, when you're not coping, awareness and insight have very little foundation to land and build on. And so it was with me, off and on, after Connor's transition.

When Connor told me: *"Please do not be sad. You must use this opportunity, this spaciousness, this time, to expand who you are on the planet,"* it didn't land, but it did speed up the process. The knowing ends the pain, but not the grief. That takes linear time, it seems; I was grieving the void that no one could ever fill, an endless pit. No one wants to stay in that hole any longer than they have to.

As I moved into retaining what I became aware of, as I clearly heard the confirmations from Sage Council and Connor 2.0 and through conversations with Cheryl, as my meditative moments became richer and deeper again, things started rolling more quickly. I began to process and integrate everything and receive confirmation on another level. I was ready to take the baton and run the next leg of the journey. I could see that clearly now.

Sage Council helped me roll it all together, to connect the dots: *"In this lifetime, Jonni, you resisted incarnating as you so loved being able to be a vibrational lightserver on the other side. You loved being pure and bodiless love, and felt that you could serve at the highest level in that form.*

When you were called to incarnate again you had free choice, as do all souls, but it was highly suggested you come back to Earth to resolve residual love blocks. The promise you made was that you would clear all earthly love blocks so that after this lifetime you could choose not to incarnate again, but to be the purest of lights in the spiritual realms.

Jonni, you and Connor resided in the same level of spiritual love and growth. What convinced you to reincarnate was the promise made by Connor to spend a large part of your time on the Earth with you. Cheryl also agreed to reunite in this soul group, and your recognition of soul-to-soul love would be gained through having Connor in your life, and then continued through your work with Sage Council.

You, Jonni, the mother of all mothers, agreed to Connor's transition time when you were in spirit form because you could see the life plan and how his exit would impact your commitment to your spiritual work. You also saw that you would need help in order to stay grounded on Earth, and that was the promise Blake made. He would keep you safe while you were in earthly form, and ensure that you would be in your body. This was one of the reasons you came back: to experience the integration and embodiment of spiritual in human form.

You and Connor have both had that "alien feeling" because you have not wanted to be part of the human collective. It feels so primitive to you both in comparison to the high remembering you have of the other realms. You have low tolerance for those who are not connected to Spirit, as you are deeply empathetic to the work that you have done previously. When those on the planet do not choose the spiritual path, it saddens you to such a degree you cannot connect with them. At the same time, part of the healing for you is to practice loving non-attachment to all beings."

What Sage Council described wasn't some kind of spiritual snobbery. I never felt superior. I only felt committed or sad. It was clearly time to stop feeling sad. That wasn't helping anyone. It was all about rising above the emotional line, as though all the fears and sadnesses and questions and worries and concerns were all in this ball of emotional stuff and I didn't need to live in it. You could say, "well, those things are life, Jonni", but it's a version of life, a channel of life, just as living higher and lighter is a version of life. If I was going to stay on the planet, I would need to integrate it better.

I noted when the Sage Council messages and confirmations moved from personal to universal. It wasn't about me anymore. It was about the modelling, the example.

"It may seem like it's been a test for capacity to love through the things that have happened in your life. When we feel that we

have been sucker punched, or that love has been taken from us, the underlining opportunity is to find the love, even in what seems to be the most loveless situations. And we know this does not provide comfort when going through the physical and human pain of a life-altering experience, but spend your moment to moment existence asking yourself, "How can I more deeply love in this moment?; What is the most loving thing to do in this moment?"

When I went through the typical stages of the grieving process, Sage Council reminded me where the anger was truly coming from.

"When Connor transitioned, you were envious and longing and frustrated that he could be in that place of freedom without you. But his role now is to help you further integrate spirit into form. Connor's purpose is to assist you from where he is. We are a lifeline, Jonni, keeping you connected to the realms you came from.

Your energy, Jonni, is attuned to high-vibration love. This does not make you more special than other beings, for there are others like you, but it does mean that your vibration has been attuned to seek love, and to share love, in higher capacities than others. The vibrations that are wired for higher-capacity love must find the place within themselves through connection to Spirit, through connection to memories of love, to be love in the majority of their moments.

The definition of hell on Earth is the purgatory of wresting with the meaning of pain. It is human to seek to understand. It is spiritual to integrate, and to seek to find peace and grace with what is."

Without the daily physical connection, I had no way of knowing what Connor was doing anymore. That may sound strange, but my human brain went back and forth from remembering, understanding and accepting, to needing to know what he was doing in the most practical way. I couldn't stretch to experience him when I was in a logical, three-dimensional headspace, so I wanted measurable facts. I didn't need to see him. He did not have a prolonged illness that wreaked havoc with his physical body, leaving an imprint on my memory that needed to be restored. He was a healthy and beautiful young man when I saw him off on his amazing journey, so my physical sense of him was robust and whole.

Sage Council shared: "*Connor wants to let you know that he is grooving on the tunes of energetic, angelic love. A typical day for him is to be in awe of the earthly sunrise and the music that goes with it. From there, he visits the trees and the ocean on the Earth, to delight in the magic that is the Earth. And from there he comes to you energetically and kisses you on the cheek, Jonni, to celebrate your human existence, and to be absolutely ecstatic with the progress that you are making on the planet Earth.*

Connor also works with the people he has made the promise to, beaming love to them in his energetic form. This is his purpose and plan in the energetic form. It is not purpose like it is on the planet. It is love grooving on love, waves and waves and waves of love. It is like being present on the Earth times one million. It is feeling the dew on a leaf on a tree. It is being the sun as it awakens to the day. It is being the moon as it reveals itself in the night sky.

Everyone who transitions is all that is. Everyone who is human is all that is. But the difference for those who have transitioned is that they can be all that is without interference, without the brain as a filter.

For now, imagine Connor 2.0 as vibrating molecularly on the grooves of love. He is attracted to where there is love. He is joined by others who are in his soul circle, and together they dance and move and merge.

Physical reality limits your ability to be pure light energy, Jonni, but Connor will be your dragonfly, if you will, and take you by the hand and fly you to all information in a very fine, fine vibration of non-emotional energy.

Jonni, you are very aligned with the truth of what's coming through and what we're looking to help expand on the planet at this time, which is to help people further access the inter-dimensional realities, and for you to be their shaman or guide or journey partner to access the wisdom and the connection to the love, and then bring it back into their lives with concrete and practical guidance. Your role, Jonni, is helping people reach high into the ethers to access the love and the truth, and then bring them through into their earthly lives so they can practice and walk and talk and be their inter-dimensional self on the planet Earth."

Over time, Sage Council began referring to Connor's transition as "the expansion". I liked that. I knew it was a transformation of Connor and a transformation of myself, so it wasn't a great leap to see the entire experience as an expansion. I was becoming more aligned with the greater truth, and consistently now.

"There is an opportunity through this expansion to bring the messaging through in more and more ways, where more and more people are glimpsing that there is no way the linear reality can be the answer to higher happiness and love.

This is an exciting time. It is an auspicious time. It is a time when the unification requires everyone to step up, not lollygag or spend time in traditional earthly psychology which anchors to victim and self, but rather elevate up to the tenets of transpersonal psychology which is about collective unification.

Jonni, we are very, very pleased at the speed with which you've accepted Connor's new reality. And although emotions are the gateway to Spirit on planetary existence, you have transmuted those emotions of loss and sadness for his physical self into the bigger promise that was made when he would go to the other side to assist you in this next level of your work.

It's actually a very, very intrinsic and extremely complex design that the universe has created where every realm has its filter of interpretation and communication. If you think of a spiral, you will see that with every spiral you go up, the communication becomes less and less emotional, and more a finer and finer connection of love message."

Nowadays, when I commune with Connor 2.0, I'm open to his non-verbal, internal messages. He connects with me most often through mind-to-mind communication, particularly when I'm walking - something we did together most evenings - or driving. At other times it's simply me, processing out loud or internally, and Connor 2.0 doing what he always used to do as Connor: letting me know he's there listening, and sharing what resonates with him. He has not come through as an external audio, or a figure. There are times when he simply downloads fully-developed ideas and concepts and I rush to scribble out the details. And there are days when he works right with me, right through me, entwined in the words, in the emotions, in the message.

The secret to my relationship with Connor 2.0 began when I released him from my desire to keep him only to myself, and only as my son. When I opened up and allowed the greater love story, the soul-to-soul love story, to be shared, the truth, as they say, sets you free.

No matter where I am on the planet, I feel Connor right beside me, lovingly cherishing me as he always has. Sage Council agrees.

"Jonni, we have a message from Connor. He wants you to know that in his multidimensional state he is able to simultaneously experience the birds and the breeze and the flow that is Hawaii, and the branches and the tree that is his tree in the snow. As he's being a snow angel, he is also being a beach angel. In his multidimensional state, he is an angel of every element.

He knows and sees that you are beautifully blossoming into your powerful self, into the promise you made to yourself that you would be in this lifetime. He wants to remind you that in the pre-incarnate state, the two of you, as beautiful lights, as souls, saw and agreed to the vision of the lifetime as mother and son on Earth and how it would play out, and with expansive energetics you both agreed to live out this choice of love path.

Connor has always seen a life of empowered self for you, Jonni - empowered to choices and well-being and love of self.

Your work is going to continue to expand and reach more, and in order for you to be able to sustain the energy required for that, you must continue your ability to self empower, to choose what is right for you, to be true to your essence. This is what Connor always wished for you when he was on the Earth, and what he sees you doing now.

Connor also wants to remind you that he is timeless and ageless and forever young."

AFTERWORD

by Cheryl

Sage Council Co-Channeller

The love and partnership between Jonni and Connor was always awe-inspiring. Not in a 'put her on a pedestal' way, but more in an "I want to be that kind of parent to my child" way. The sacredness of their bond was palpable then, as it is now. I can't think of another person who mothered with her knowledge of spirit and connection. Beautiful connection. There is such depth of love there. Connor's leaving is a legacy of that love.

The journey Jonni and I are on as soul sisters who reconnected in this lifetime to carry forward our promise to serve and share love, has been a divine gift. When Jonni and I met, we immediately knew each other, and over the years have remained connected through the work we do with Sage Council. Each time we connect to channel the energy of love messages from Sage Council, we are infused with deep love.

Over the years we have learned to bring this love to our lives, and recently, to the lives of others.

Connor always knew, and always had, the energetic knowing of universal love. It was in his being from birth, as it is for all souls. He also had a mother in Jonni who had the loving awareness to help him nurture his knowing.

What a gift of a soul Connor was and is. He would delight at a sunrise, and jump for joy at the beauty of nature, and share his love and joy with all. Isn't that what love is about? Don't we need models of love like Connor and Jonni to show us how it can be?

This book is a love story, but not love in the way many see it to be. It is the big love, the only real love, the love that is what is. Please open your heart and let the big love in.

AFTERWORD

by Sage Council

"What is a conduit? A circle of love. A pathway of love. Through eternity in the energetic realm, we have always held, and do hold, the glue of the universe: love. Love is the organizer. It is the matter; it is the gravity; it is the no-matter; it is the free, open space. It is the molecules that make up all physical matter that is viewed by the human eye. It is the space between the matter. Everything in the universe is of an energetic scale. At certain levels on the energetic scale, there is the ability to be a conduit, a route, or a pathway from Earth to Spirit.

The physical being known as Connor was an innate conduit, which means he came into his birth, and into his life on the planet, knowing that this was his purpose. His purpose was to bring love, and to show others how to be love, through the physical form. He did this for his mother, Jonni. He did this for his father. He did this for the teachers in his schools. He did this for his friends, and he did this for anyone he connected with.

The earthly plane has transition points for all of you who chose to incarnate. Every human being on the planet chooses optional exit points in their life. Connor, as a conduit, chose to exit at a time when he could say, with full love, "My work here is done". His work in helping his mother, his father, his friends, and everyone he connected with, was done, and he was called to be in the energetic realm where he could expand his work a million-fold.

The link between Jonni and Connor is a true soulmate link and relationship: soul-to-soul promise in many lifetimes, soul-to-soul promise in this lifetime, teacher-student/student-teacher, leader of love/follower of love. It did not matter that the earthly roles were mother and son, the soul story transcends those identities. Timeless love, spiritual love, the love that is authentic to universal congruence, is the love that binds all, and in Jonni and Connor's case, it was a love that they knew and remembered and honoured in this lifetime, and beyond this lifetime, even still.

The beauty of this book being birthed right now through Jonni is the wonderful love story. It is not the love story you see as humans in the movies or in books, but a love story of before, during, and after physical earthly life. It is a love story that causes everyone who reads it to know that there is love, available and always permeating, always accessible, and <u>that</u> love is the love you must seek as true love.

This book models authentic relationship: relationship with integrity that was based on soul understanding. It is a model for how relationships can be, and how we, as Sage Council on the energetic side, want relationships to be. This does not mean that Jonni and Connor did not have earthly challenges. However, the glue that consistently held them and holds them is the deep and intimate trust in sacred, universal love. It is that intimate and sacred trust in universal love that creates authentic connection with all.

The identities that each of you have on the planet - mother, father, uncle, aunt, brother, sister, wife, husband - are not roles that are indicators of soul-based love. They are roles.

If humans become attached to the identities, they confuse love with obligation. Soul-centred relationships are about honouring the love that is behind, and permeates through, earthly expressions of love. Soul-centred relationships are about loving someone for who they are, seeing their soul version of self and accepting that as who they are, trusting soul-guided messages from each other, communing soul-to-soul through meditation as Jonni and Connor did, and through guided dialogue on the realities beyond physical manifestation.

We urged Jonni to write this book. We urged her to share this divine love story, not as an ideal above any other relationship that exists, but as a story of soul-to-soul love. Expand your heart and connect to the energy of this story. Make a promise to live your life with a deeper committed awareness of universal, soul-sacred love."